John
A Devotional Commentary

BOB ROGNLIEN

DEDICATION

To my sons Bobby and Luke.
I love you and I'm so proud of the husbands, fathers,
and followers of Jesus you have become.
You are the apple of my eye,
the joy of my heart,
and the crown of my life.

ACKNOWLEDGEMENTS

I want to express my gratitude to all those who supported me, prayed for me, and made the writing of this book and series possible. Specifically, I want to thank Pam Rognlien, Chris Pudel, and Heidi Hollings for carefully rooting out my many mistakes. Any which remain are mine alone. Thanks to Robert Neely for editing the manuscript and Amit Dey for designing the interior pages. They have both made the book eminently more readable. Special thanks to Tim Bergren for designing another great book cover. Above all I give thanks to Jesus, the Great Shepherd of the Sheep, who continues inviting us all to listen to his voice and follow him by taking steps of faith every day. To him be all the glory!

INTRODUCTION

In the first chapter of his Gospel, Mark describes Jesus' predictable pattern of spending time alone with his heavenly Father the King. *Very early in the morning, while it was still dark, he got up, went out, and made his way to a deserted place; and there he was praying.* (Mark 1:35)

Those who follow Jesus recognize this is a critical rhythm of discipleship, seeking to become more like him by hearing and responding to what he is saying every day. Paul says, *"So faith comes from what is heard, and what is heard comes through the message about Christ."* (Romans 10:17) When we listen for the voice of Jesus speaking through his written Word, the Holy Spirit plants faith in our hearts. When we exercise that faith by taking a concrete step in the footsteps of Jesus, we grow as his fruitful disciples and learn to live a more Jesus-shaped life.

Footsteps Every Day is a series of devotional commentaries on the New Testament, designed to help followers of Jesus establish a regular pattern of spending time alone with God, reading Scripture, listening in prayer, and responding with a step of faith. Volume Four, *John,* is the fourth in the series and offers brief reflections on 73 passages that make up John's account of Jesus' life, drawing on history, archaeology, and culture to illuminate the Way of Jesus and help you follow him with concrete steps of faith.

Each of these devotional commentaries can be read on its own at your own pace, or you can read all four Gospels in succession. If you read six passages a week, the first four volumes will take you on an incredible year-long journey through the Gospels, following the life of Jesus and reflecting on every recorded thing he said and did during his life on earth!

These books can also be used as biblical commentaries by looking up a specific passage you are studying to gain fresh insights from the historical and cultural background to inform you as you teach others and apply God's Word to daily life.

Here are my recommendations for a fruitful devotional journey in Jesus' *Footsteps Every Day*:

- Pick a time in which you have the highest likelihood of being consistent each day. Set aside at least 15 minutes, or better 30 minutes.

- Pick a place where you will be the least distracted and interrupted. Make yourself comfortable but adopt an attentive posture. Get too comfortable and you will fall asleep!

- Read the Scripture passage in your own Bible. My writing is based on the text from the Christian Standard Bible, an excellent and often overlooked translation, but you can use any version you find helpful. Read it again.

- Take some time to prayerfully listen as you scan over the passage, noting what God seems to be pointing out to you.

- Highlight important phrases and make relevant notes in the margins. (Even digital Bibles allow for this. I use the Olive Tree App.)

- Read the commentary provided in *Footsteps Every Day*.

- Prayerfully ask God what he is saying to you through all the above. Listen and write down what is coming to you in the space provided (or type it as a digital note if you are reading the eBook edition).

- Then ask God to show you the next step of faith he wants you to take.

- Write down your step of faith in the space provided (or type it as a digital note if you are reading the eBook edition).

- Take that step of faith!

- If you are having trouble taking that step, share it with someone you trust and ask them to pray for you to exercise the faith God is giving you. Take that step of faith!

- Rinse and repeat!

- At the end of every six days, there is a section called "Footsteps Every Week." Use this space to reflect on the readings from the past week, summarize your insights from each day, identify any major themes, consider any new predictable patterns God is calling you to establish, and identify the most significant verse to memorize.

When we read God's Word and listen to what Jesus is saying to us through the Spirit, it produces faith in our hearts. Our role is to respond to what Jesus is saying by exercising that faith, taking the next step in following the footsteps of Jesus. We are not trying to change ourselves by moral willpower, but rather are putting ourselves in the place where God's Spirit can transform us from the inside out. This is what it means to live as a Jesus-shaped disciple. Please don't approach this as a religious task that you must perform but receive this opportunity as a gracious invitation to draw near to Jesus, hear his voice, and follow where he leads you on this great adventure of discipleship!

DAY 1

READ AND LISTEN: JOHN 1:1-13

Take a minute to listen for what God is saying in these verses…

COMMENT AND CONSIDER

John and his brother James, sons of Zebedee, lived in Capernaum on the north shore of the Sea of Galilee. They worked in their extended family's fishing business in partnership with Simon and Andrew's family. James and John's mother was Salome, most likely a sister of Mary the mother of Jesus, which would make them Jesus' cousins. (Compare Matthew 27:56, Mark 15:40, and John 19:25.) John must have had a bold personality, because once these brothers asked Jesus for permission to call down *"fire from heaven"* on some inhospitable Samaritans. (Luke 9:54) No wonder Jesus nicknamed them *"Sons of Thunder."* (Mark 3:17)

John's family must have come from Jerusalem originally, because he demonstrates more detailed knowledge of the Holy City than the other Gospel writers. He was also an *"acquaintance of the high priest,"* able to gain access to Caiaphas' courtyard. (John 18:15) If the exceptional literary skill reflected in his Gospel and letters is any indication, John may have had an advanced education. Along with James and Peter, John was one of Jesus' three closest disciples who sometimes accompanied him on special ventures, such as climbing the Mount of Transfiguration and praying in the Garden of Gethsemane. (See Mark 9:2,14:33.)

John, along with Peter, became one of the most influential of the apostolic leaders, eventually overseeing all the churches in Ephesus and the surrounding region, which became the most significant center of Christian mission in the early church. While he was in Ephesus, he wrote the fourth Gospel and the three letters of John. Eventually, he was exiled by the Romans to the remote island of Patmos, where he received and recorded Revelation, the final book of the New Testament.

John's account of Jesus' life and mission is markedly different from the other three Gospels in both outline and content. It's as if John intentionally set out to give us a different perspective on Jesus, while confirming the broad outlines of the earlier Gospels. He follows the overall framework of Jesus' life from birth to baptism to public ministry in Galilee, celebrating the final Passover in Jerusalem, arrest, condemnation, execution, and resurrection. But unlike the other three accounts of Jesus' life, often called the Synoptic ("same view") Gospels, John tells us about five trips Jesus made to Jerusalem for festivals during the course of his ministry. He describes seven miraculous *"signs"* Jesus performed and seven *"I am"* statements, all of which point us to Jesus' true identity as the fully divine and fully incarnate Son of God.

John begins his account of Jesus' life masterfully with one of the most beautiful and profound poems in all of Scripture, the Logos Prologue. Evoking the opening lines of Genesis 1, John tells us Jesus' birth constitutes a new beginning for all people, the genesis of a New Creation. John doesn't just begin with the birth of Jesus, as Matthew and Luke do, but reaches all the way back before the beginning of time to show us how Jesus, in his full divinity, existed before all things and was the very agent of creation when God first spoke the whole universe into existence out of nothing.

To explain this John draws on the popular language of Stoic philosophy, which used the Greek word *logos,* translated "Word," to describe the one divine principle and intelligence that transcends all things and holds all things together. John tells us Jesus is the true Logos whose light of life scatters the darkness to fully reveal God to us. He introduces us to John the Baptist, who testified to the light of life in Jesus so we can receive him, believe in him, and be born into a new identity and family as the daughters and sons of God.

What does it mean to you that Jesus is fully God and fully human at the same time? Do you believe in him? Have you received him? What does it mean to be born into the family of God?

REFLECT AND RESPOND

What is Jesus saying to me right now?

What step of faith is Jesus calling me to take today?

DAY 2

READ AND LISTEN: JOHN 1:14-28

Take a minute to listen for what God is saying in these verses…

COMMENT AND CONSIDER

John concludes his profound poetic description of Jesus the Logos by moving from the cosmic to the concrete: *"The Word became flesh and dwelt among us."* The preexisting Word of God, who called all things into being out of nothing, entered the very universe he created and became part of the creation. As the definitive Son of the Father, Jesus revealed the glory of God by embodying him in this world in a way that people could see with their own eyes, hear with their own ears, and touch with their own hands. This divine glory was manifested in both the freely given gift of total acceptance, along with an unwavering expression of the way things really are. *"We observed his glory, the glory as the one and only Son from the Father, full of grace and truth."*

The grace that came through Jesus is not a denial of our sin and shame. His truth brings to light that which is hidden. But what is revealed is not cause for condemnation, because sin is dealt with and shame is wiped away. The Law as interpreted by the Pharisees offered truth without grace and so delivered guilt and condemnation. At the other end of the spectrum, the Sadducees focused on maintaining the sacrificial rituals of the Temple so they could offer absolution regardless of the state of people's hearts and lives, offering grace without truth. By contrast Jesus came to bring both grace and truth, both the diagnosis and the cure. *"Indeed, we have all received grace upon grace from his fullness, for the law was given through Moses; grace and truth came through Jesus Christ."*

When the scribes and Pharisees paraded a woman caught in the very act of adultery before Jesus, they held in their hands the stones of condemnation. Truth without grace. Apparently, they were not concerned about the man who bore equal if not greater responsibility in that patriarchal society. Grace without truth. They asked Jesus what he would do, and he simply replied,

"The one without sin among you should be the first to throw a stone at her." Once they all dropped their stones and walked away, he said to the woman, *"Go, and from now on do not sin anymore."* (John 8:7-11) Full of grace. Full of truth.

John records the testimony of John the Baptist, whose fiery sermons and immersion baptisms stirred up controversy and questions. The Temple authorities sent priests and Levites to investigate John. The Pharisees also sent representatives to find out who John really was. Was he Elijah, who was taken up to heaven, now returned as God had promised? (See 2 Kings 2:11 and Malachi 4:5.) Was he the Prophet like Moses that God had promised to send? (See Deuteronomy 18:15–18.) Or was he the Messiah, the anointed king descended from David, come to establish God's eternal Kingdom? (See 2 Samuel 7:11-16.)

John was crystal clear, *"I am not the Messiah."* When they pressed him to identify himself, he said, *"I am a voice of one crying out in the wilderness: Make straight the way of the Lord—just as Isaiah the prophet said."* His call for people to be immersed in the waters of the Jordan River was a call to repentance, to a change of heart and mind. This is how he prepared the way for the coming of the Messiah; he was preparing their hearts and minds to receive him. John did not yet know his cousin Jesus was the one whose way he was preparing, but he prophesied the divine nature of the Messiah when he said, *"The one coming after me ranks ahead of me, because he existed before me."* John knew his role. He was to prepare the way and then get out of the way when the Messiah came.

Does it matter that God became flesh in Jesus? Do you tend to be full of grace or full of truth? Are you more prone to pick up a stone or drop one? Can you describe God's purpose for your life? How can you prepare the way for Jesus?

REFLECT AND RESPOND

What is Jesus saying to me right now?

What step of faith is Jesus calling me to take today?

DAY 3

READ AND LISTEN: JOHN 1:29-42

Take a minute to listen for what God is saying in these verses…

COMMENT AND CONSIDER

John the Baptist was the only son of elderly parents, Zechariah and Elizabeth, who lived in the hill country of Judea outside of Jerusalem. Zechariah was a priest who served in the Temple for one week twice a year. Elizabeth was a relative of Mary the mother of Jesus, which means John and Jesus were cousins and may have played together as kids when Jesus' family made their annual pilgrimage to Jerusalem for the Passover. Luke says of the young John, *The child grew up and became strong in spirit, and he was in the wilderness until the day of his public appearance to Israel.* (Luke 1:80)

Because his parents were elderly and probably died when he was still young, John may have been adopted by the Essenes, who built a community in the desert wilderness at Qumran on the northwest shore of the Dead Sea. Josephus tells us adoption was an Essene practice to help continue their community, because many of them did not marry. Since John had so much in common with the Essene community and carried out his public ministry so close to Qumran, it seems likely there was some connection between them. If he was a member of the Essene community at Qumran, it may be that he was expelled for disagreeing with their teaching of two Messiahs or their obsession with ritual purity, which could have sparked his mission.

John's ministry drew a lot of attention and people of every social class and background came to hear him preach and be baptized in the Jordan River. John's clothing and diet was reminiscent of the prophet Elijah, and he operated as a classic prophet, speaking on behalf of God to the people. When John saw Jesus coming to him for baptism, he suddenly realized his cousin was the one for whom he had been preparing! John prophesied, *"Look, the Lamb of God, who takes away the sin of the world!"* It is hard to imagine a more insightful statement about the person and purpose of Jesus before his mission had even begun!

When John the Baptist said this again the next day, two of his disciples, Andrew and an unnamed disciple (probably John), decided they needed to get to know this Jesus better. So they began to follow him, dropping hints for an invitation. Jesus obliged them, inviting them to join him where he was staying. They picked up Simon on the way and spent the rest of the day with Jesus. Since it was four in the afternoon, Jesus was culturally obligated to offer them dinner and a place to sleep for the night.

In his very first engagement with others, we see Jesus implementing the strategy he later trained his disciples to use in carrying out their mission to seek and save the lost. In Luke 10 Jesus told his followers to go out in pairs, offer their friendship to others, see who would receive and reciprocate that invitation, and then invest in those relationships, first showing and then telling them the Good News of the Kingdom. Here we see Jesus offering his friendship to Andrew, Simon, and John by welcoming them, listening to them, and serving them. When Jesus returned to Capernaum, after being rejected by his hometown and extended family, he discovered Simon and Andrew were ready to reciprocate his invitation to friendship by welcoming him into their extended family home where they listened to him and served him. From that point on, Jesus invested everything he had in them, producing incredibly fruitful leaders in the Kingdom he was building.

Jesus shows us how to reach the lost, make disciples, and bring the Kingdom of God to life: find friends who will serve you, call followers who will submit to you, and build families that are surrendered to the will of God. Are you open to the surprising insights the Holy Spirit might bring to you through prophecy? What does it mean for you to embrace Jesus as the Lamb of God? How are you going about your mission? Are you following the same strategy Jesus used?

REFLECT AND RESPOND

What is Jesus saying to me right now?

What step of faith is Jesus calling me to take today?

DAY 4

READ AND LISTEN: JOHN 1:43-51

Take a minute to listen for what God is saying in these verses…

COMMENT AND CONSIDER

As Jesus prepared to depart from the Jordan River and return to his hometown in Galilee, he met a man named Philip. Jews of the Diaspora, who had left the land of Israel to live elsewhere in the Roman Empire, often had both a Hebrew and a Roman name. The Pharisee Saul of Tarsus whose Roman name was Paul is a well-known example. Philip is a Greek name which would be somewhat unusual for a Jew living in Palestine, but John tells us he came from Bethsaida, a fishing village on the north shore of the Sea of Galilee. Recent excavations have confirmed the location of Bethsaida, east of where the River Jordan entered the lake in the territory ruled by Herod Philip, half-brother of Herod Antipas, tetrarch of Galilee. Among the recent finds is a first-century bathhouse, demonstrating the extent of Roman cultural influence on this primarily Jewish village.

Herod Philip was particularly fond of Greek culture and in AD 30 elevated the official status of Bethsaida to the rank of a *polis* (Greek for "city") and renamed it "Julias" in honor of Livia, the wife of the late Roman Emperor Augustus, whose formal title was Julia Augusta. So, it is not surprising that a Jew from Bethsaida-Julias in Herod Philip's territory would have a Greek name- Philip. John's statement that Bethsaida was also the hometown of Andrew and Peter is a hint they were the ones who introduced Philip to Jesus. We know Peter and Andrew lived in Capernaum, just to the west of Bethsaida, but apparently they had moved their extended family and fishing business there from their original hometown, Bethsaida.

It is startling that Jesus called Philip as a disciple immediately after their first meeting. Students who excelled in primary school, called *Beth Sefer,* could apply for further studies in *Beth Midrash.* The best students could then apply to become a disciple of the rabbi, living and traveling with their teacher. The decision of the rabbi to accept a student who had applied to become one of his disciples was based on years of demonstrated skill and dedication.

Jesus was radically counter-cultural in calling blue-collar workers with only basic primary education as his disciples, since they did not qualify and would never presume to even apply for this elite position. When Jesus said to Philip, *"Follow me,"* Philip was so moved by this shocking invitation he immediately found his friend Nathanael who came from Cana, a Jewish town west of the Sea of Galilee near Nazareth, and told him, *"We have found the one Moses wrote about in the law (and so did the prophets): Jesus the son of Joseph, from Nazareth."* Nathanael responded rather cynically, *"Can anything good come out of Nazareth?"*

Modern Nazareth overlooks the Jezreel Valley in Galilee and has over 70,000 inhabitants, the largest city in Israel with a primarily Arab population. However, in the time of Jesus it was a small, rural village of perhaps 800-1,000 conservative, religious Jewish residents. There is no reference to Nazareth in the Old Testament, attesting to its relative insignificance. Nathanael's statement was not an indictment of Nazareth's immorality, but instead testimony to its unimportance! Philip responded by simply challenging him to come meet Jesus for himself.

When Jesus first saw Nathanael he declared, *"Here truly is an Israelite in whom there is no deceit,"* and then went on to explain that he had seen Nathanael sitting under a fig tree. Nathanael knew there was no human way Jesus could have known these things about him and exclaimed, *"You are the Son of God; you are the King of Israel!"* Jesus chided Nathanael that this was the least of the miracles he was going to witness if he followed him.

What moved Philip and Nathanael to respond to Jesus with such enthusiastic faith? How are you responding to Jesus? Are you as enthusiastic as Philip about introducing your friends to Jesus?

REFLECT AND RESPOND

What is Jesus saying to me right now?

What step of faith is Jesus calling me to take today?

DAY 5

Read and Listen: John 2:1-11

Take a minute to listen for what God is saying in these verses…

Comment and Consider

Until recently there has been uncertainty about the location of Cana, but the discovery of an altar with places for six stone jars in a cave where early Christians worshiped has clarified that Khirbet Cana is the correct site. Cana was a Jewish village situated on a hill overlooking the Natofa Valley, about 8 miles northeast of Nazareth. It was the hometown of Nathanael, introduced to us in the verses immediately preceding this account, which may indicate the source of this wedding invitation. Jewish wedding celebrations in the first century, one of the most important events in the life of an extended family, often lasted an entire week. It was the responsibility of the groom's family to host the celebrations and provide food and drink.

Middle Eastern culture is based on maximizing honor and minimizing shame. Whatever brings the greatest positive recognition to me, my family, and others is the highest priority. Whatever causes us to be disparaged by others is to be avoided at all costs. Hospitality is one of the highest values in this cultural context. Welcoming people of honor into your home and providing more than they need is absolutely critical. Thus, it was a major crisis for the groom's family when they discovered their supply of wine was running out!

The fact that Mary informed Jesus of the crisis indicates she may have been related to the hosts. Jesus' response tells us she assumed he could do something to avert the crisis. Jesus' response was not rude, as the abrupt response *woman* sounds in English. This was actually a term of respect more like "ma'am." However, Jesus made it clear to his mother that she was not directing his decisions anymore. As the Synoptic Gospels point out, Mary did not yet understand the true nature of Jesus' Messianic mission. (See Mark 3:20-21, 6:4 and Luke 4:16-30.)

Despite setting this boundary with his mother, Jesus responded to the crisis and ordered the servants to fill six stone jars used to hold water for purification with water. The rabbis taught that pottery could not be ritually purified once defiled, but stone vessels could be symbolically cleansed. These six large stone water jars in their home tells us the hosts were Law-observant Jews and also people of significant means. Expensive stone jars just like these, only slightly smaller, have been discovered by archaeologists in first-century homes of wealthy, priestly families in Jerusalem.

Headwaiter was a respected position filled by someone of social influence (like a Master of Ceremonies) who supervised the music, entertainment, and refreshments at a banquet. One of his responsibilities was to monitor the dilution of the wine to prevent excess drunkenness. Since water supplies were nearly always unclean in the ancient Middle East, drinking water was normally disinfected with one part wine to three parts water. For a wedding celebration that could stretch on for several days, the festivities normally began with full-strength wine served to impress the guests, followed by increasing levels of dilution as the party went on. Either the correct supply of wine was not delivered, or the headwaiter did not properly dilute the wine.

In any case, Jesus told the servants to draw from the contents of the stone jars and bring the liquid to the headwaiter for tasting. Galilee was the major wine-producing region of Palestine with a wide range of wines of varying quality available. It was natural for families hosting a banquet to serve the best wine first, then serve a lower-quality vintage once the dilution had begun. But when he tasted the wine, the headwaiter was shocked the hosts had held back the finest vintage for later in the evening! As this miraculous wine was served, not only was the host family saved from utter humiliation, but their honor grew in the eyes of their community.

How do you respond when others are in danger of being publicly ridiculed? Are you willing to step in and protect those who might be subject to unwarranted shame? Are you willing to look foolish yourself to protect others?

REFLECT AND RESPOND

What is Jesus saying to me right now?

What step of faith is Jesus calling me to take today?

DAY 6

READ AND LISTEN: JOHN 2:12-25

Take a minute to listen for what God is saying in these verses…

COMMENT AND CONSIDER

The outline of Jesus' life is consistent in all four Gospels: baptism in the Jordan River, teaching and healing centered in Galilee, a final Passover in Jerusalem followed by arrest, sham trials, crucifixion, and resurrection. However, each Gospel writer organized their record of what Jesus said and did differently, not necessarily chronologically. John weaves seven *signs* and seven *I am statements* throughout his narrative, including five trips from Galilee to Jerusalem where he taught in the Temple courts during the Jewish festivals of Passover, Booths, and Dedication. Three of these trips were for the Passover, which is why we typically estimate the length of Jesus' public mission to be around three years.

In John's first account of Jesus traveling to Jerusalem for the Passover, he describes Jesus' shocking act of overturning the tables of the money changers and driving out those who were selling animals. This would have been perceived as a direct challenge to the authority of the High Priest Caiaphas and the Chief Priests, whose authority was rooted in the sacrificial system. Did this radical demonstration happen near the beginning or the end of Jesus' public ministry? Matthew, Mark, and Luke place this provocative act near the end of Jesus' ministry, which cements the determination of the threatened religious leaders to have him put to death. By putting this event at the beginning of Jesus' ministry, John infuses the entirety of his narrative with the direct conflict between Jesus and the religious leaders.

Which is the historically correct chronology? We could argue the clearing of the Temple makes the most sense at the end of Jesus' ministry because it fueled the religious leaders' plan to have Jesus executed. However, since it was Jesus' lifelong pattern to attend the Passover in Jerusalem (see Luke 2:41), and one year seems too short for Jesus to accomplish all that is recorded, it follows that John must be correct in recording three Passovers in Jerusalem. Since the Synoptic Gospels, only record one trip to Jerusalem, perhaps they combined earlier events into this single visit at the end of his ministry, including the clearing of the Temple. Another possibility is that Jesus carried out this provocative act twice, once at the beginning and again at the end of his ministry, but this seems the least likely solution.

Regardless of when Jesus carried out this provocative act, we still have to wrestle with why he did it and what it means. Jesus' cry, *"Stop turning my Father's house into a marketplace!"* tells us the Temple leadership was corrupt, using power to serve themselves and fill their own coffers. But if Jesus was trying to reform the practice of buying and selling on the Temple Mount, it would have caused a disturbance large enough to provoke the Roman army to deploy from the Antonia Fortress, which was built over the northwest corner of the Temple courts, as they did when a crowd accused Paul of bringing a Gentile into the inner courts of the Temple. (See Acts 21:26-36.) Since no soldiers deployed from the Antonia Fortress to stop Jesus, we can conclude this was a relatively limited action, not affecting every money changer and animal seller in the Temple courts.

If Jesus was not trying to reform Temple practice, what was the point of his action? Biblical prophets often performed shocking symbolic acts to symbolize God's judgment of his people. God told Jeremiah to smash a pot as a symbol of impending destruction and then told him to announce that judgment in the courts of the Temple. (See Jeremiah 19:1-15.) Jesus carried out a similar prophetic act of judgment against the religious leaders of Jerusalem who would soon see this enormous Temple complex completely destroyed by the Romans, never to be rebuilt again. He was also making a prophetic statement about his own body, which would be destroyed and rebuilt in three days.

Are you able to discern the warning signs that call for repentance, or do you tend to get defensive and deflect judgment onto others? Are you willing to warn others of the destructive consequences of their actions even if it makes people uncomfortable? How do you balance this with a message of grace and forgiveness?

REFLECT AND RESPOND

What is Jesus saying to me right now?

What step of faith is Jesus calling me to take today?

FOOTSTEPS EVERY WEEK: REVIEW

Write a brief summary of what Jesus said to you each day this past week and the step of faith he called you to take:

MONDAY

TUESDAY

WEDNESDAY

THURSDAY

FRIDAY

SATURDAY

FOOTSTEPS EVERY WEEK: REFLECT

BIG PICTURE

As you look over what Jesus has said to you this past week, do you see any themes? What is the most important thing you need to remember and believe?

PREDICTABLE PATTERN

As you look over what Jesus called you to do this past week, is there a new predictable pattern he is inviting you to establish in your life with God and others?

PLANT THE WORD

As you look over the readings from this past week, write out the passage that feels most important for you and memorize it over the next week:

DAY 7

READ AND LISTEN: JOHN 3:1-13

Take a minute to listen for what God is saying in these verses…

COMMENT AND CONSIDER

The Jewish historian Josephus records the deeds of a rich and powerful first-century resident of Jerusalem named Buni ben Gurion and nicknamed Nicodemus, meaning "victor of the people." He was respected for his wisdom and holiness, opposed the Zealots in their rebellion against Rome, and tried to negotiate peace with the Roman general, Titus. It is possible this Nicodemus is the same man John describes coming to Jesus at night. John tells us Nicodemus was a Pharisee and a member of the Sanhedrin, the ruling council of Jerusalem, but he hid his interest in Jesus by coming to him under the cover of darkness. In the ancient world, people did not normally go out at night unless they were in a crisis or committing a crime.

Nicodemus was drawn to Jesus because of the miraculous *"signs"* he had been performing. He concluded Jesus must have *"come from God"* in order to operate in this kind of supernatural power. Jesus responded by explaining the only way to enter into God's Kingdom was to be *"born again."* This phrase can be translated "born from above" as well as "born again." John loves to use phrases with dual meanings in order to tease out the deeper truth of Jesus' teaching. To be born again we must be transformed by the power of God from one way of being into another. This is how we can begin to see and live in the Kingdom of God.

Despite being a biblical scholar and teacher, Nicodemus misunderstood Jesus and wondered how it was possible to enter again into his mother's womb to be born again! This gave Jesus an opportunity to explain further, *"Truly I tell you, unless someone is born of water and the Spirit, he cannot enter the kingdom of God."* This was reminiscent of what God said through the prophet Ezekiel, *"I will also sprinkle clean water on you, and you will be clean. I will cleanse you from all your impurities and all your idols. I will give you a new heart and put a new spirit within you; I will remove your heart of stone and give you a heart of flesh."* (Ezekiel 36:25-26)

Jesus pointed back to his own baptism by John as the entry point into a whole new way of life in the Kingdom. In contrast to his ministry of immersing people in the waters of the Jordan, John the Baptist said, *"one who is more powerful than I is coming. I am not worthy to untie the strap of his sandals. He will baptize you with the Holy Spirit and fire."* (Luke 3:16) Jesus told Nicodemus that through being immersed in both water and the Holy Spirit we are birthed from one reality into a completely new way of being by receiving a brand-new heart.

Jesus illustrates for Nicodemus how the transforming work of the Spirit is not in our control, nor is it always obvious. *"The wind blows where it pleases, and you hear its sound, but you don't know where it comes from or where it is going. So it is with everyone born of the Spirit."* Nicodemus demonstrated Jesus' point by expressing his inability to comprehend what Jesus was saying by his own wisdom. It is a reminder that mere human wisdom cannot contain the transcendent truth of God. Despite all his study and scholarship, Nicodemus could not even understand the basic starting point of the new life Jesus offered. As Jesus said, *"Whatever is born of the flesh is flesh, and whatever is born of the Spirit is spirit."* Nicodemus needed the wind of the Spirit to blow through his soul to bring a rebirth from above that his own religious study and efforts could never achieve!

Do you recognize that your own learning and efforts can only get you so far without the Spirit of God transforming you from the inside out? Are you open to the work the Holy Spirit wants to do in your life right now? Can you recognize and respond to the Spirit who moves mysteriously like the wind?

REFLECT AND RESPOND

What is Jesus saying to me right now?

What step of faith is Jesus calling me to take today?

DAY 8

READ AND LISTEN: JOHN 3:14-21

Take a minute to listen for what God is saying in these verses…

COMMENT AND CONSIDER

When the people of Israel wandered in the Sinai wilderness, they were punished for their complaining by a plague of poisonous snakes. The Lord told Moses to make a bronze snake, mount it on a pole, and lift it up so the bitten could look on it and be healed. (See Numbers 21:4-9.) Egyptians sometimes wore the image of a small snake as an amulet to ward off snake bites. At the copper mines of Timna, just north of Sinai, archaeologists found a number of copper snakes from this time used in worship of the Egyptian god Hathor, patron deity of artisans.

Jesus drew upon this unusual episode in Israel's history to make a word play on the phrase *"lifted up,"* referring to both his execution and his glorification. God makes a similar play on words through Isaiah, *"See, my servant will be successful; he will be raised and lifted up and greatly exalted. Just as many were appalled at you—his appearance was so disfigured that he did not look like a man, and his form did not resemble a human being…"* (Isaiah 52:13-14) Jesus fulfilled this prophecy by being nailed to a crossbeam, lifted and hung up on a post, disfigured and contemptible. As the snake lifted up on a pole restored life to the people of Israel, so the lifting up of Jesus on the cross, and then his glorious resurrection and ascension, brings eternal life to all humanity!

John explains how that gift of eternal life comes to us. The phrase *"God so loved"* does not describe how much God loves us, but rather the way in which God demonstrated his great love for us. The CSB translation captures this meaning with the words, *"For God loved the world in this way…"* This is how God enacted his saving love for every person on the planet, by giving his only Son as a sacrifice for our sin.

There are four Greek words which we translate "love" in English: *storge, eros, philia,* and *agape.* Each can be used as a noun or a verb. *Storge* describes the natural affection between family members. *Eros* describes the passionate attraction between lovers. *Philia* describes the mutual attraction and appreciation between friends. *Agape* describes the kind of unconditional self-giving love that moves someone to make sacrifices for another. *Storge* is rarely used in the New Testament, and *Eros* does not appear at all. *Philia* is used forty-five times in the New Testament, but *agape* is used three-hundred and twenty times!

Agape is very rarely used in classical Greek literature before the time of Jesus, so the writers of the New Testament chose this word to describe the unique love that God demonstrated for us in the life of Jesus. In this passage John captures the very essence of God's saving love for us by lifting up Jesus' willingness to die on the cross as the ultimate expression of this self-giving love. It is most significant that this saving love is offered, not just to the people of Israel, but to the whole world. This is the message of universal salvation that Jesus shared from the beginning of his public ministry in Nazareth. This was always God's plan, although the people of Israel lost sight of it. (See Luke 4:16-30.)

Jesus told us this saving love of God comes to all people by believing in him. The Greek word for believing used here, *pisteuo,* is the verbal form of the noun for "faith," *pisitis.* This means believing is more than just giving our intellectual assent to the truth of Jesus, but also putting our personal trust in him and following his way, one step of faith at a time. By following the way of Jesus and trusting the truth of Jesus, we begin to live an abundant Jesus-shaped life, beginning now and continuing for all eternity!

Are you looking to Jesus, lifted up on the cross and lifted up to heaven, to save you? Are you receiving his incredible *agape* love for you? Are you trusting Jesus by following his way and not just agreeing with his truth?

REFLECT AND RESPOND

What is Jesus saying to me right now?

What step of faith is Jesus calling me to take today?

DAY 9

READ AND LISTEN: JOHN 3:22-36

Take a minute to listen for what God is saying in these verses…

COMMENT AND CONSIDER

Jesus launched his public ministry by going to John at the Jordan River, just east of Jericho, to be baptized by his cousin. After that John continued his ministry of preaching and baptizing because Herod Antipas had not yet imprisoned him in the huge Machaerus fortress on the east side of the Dead Sea. But the Jordan River was not the only place John baptized; he also carried out his ministry in other places such as, *"Aenon near Salim."* Archaeologists believe this is the modern site known as Ainun, just north of Sychar where Jesus met the Samaritan woman at Jacob's well in the very next passage. (See John 4:1- 42.) Although there is no standing water in Ainun now, plentiful springs in the area fed pools of water suitable for ritual bathing in the first century.

Jesus and his disciples also baptized people in the Judean countryside, further south. John clarifies that Jesus wasn't doing the actual baptizing, but his disciples were. (See John 4:2.) When the disciples of John started to face opposition, they blamed Jesus for drawing people away from their ministry. When they complained about this to John, he reframed their perspective by pointing out this ministry was not something they created, but something given to them by God.

John went on to remind them he had clearly testified he was not the Messiah but was simply preparing the way for the one who was to come. In Jewish tradition the *shoshbin* was the groom's best man who was responsible for offering speeches of encouragement at the wedding, serving as a witness to the marriage, contributing financially to the cost of the celebration, and retaining evidence of the bride's virginity. John told his disciples Jesus was the groom and he was simply the *shoshbin,* responsible for supporting his friend and finding joy in him being the center of attention. This is why John wasn't worried about the crowds beginning to flock to Jesus rather than him. His joy was complete because he knew, *"He must increase, but I must decrease."*

John the Gospel writer goes on to echo John the Baptist's sentiments. He knows he is simply offering his earthly testimony to the heavenly reality of Jesus, who is so much greater and more important than he is. *"The one who is from the earth is earthly and speaks in earthly terms. The one who comes from heaven is above all."* John is giving his earthly testimony of what he saw and experienced as Jesus' disciple, but he is also recording the heavenly testimony of Jesus who taught them the far greater things he saw and experienced. Jesus' testimony is the revelation John wants us to heed, far more than his own.

John goes on to explain why Jesus' testimony is so powerful. *"For the one whom God sent speaks God's words, since he gives the Spirit without measure."* When John the Baptist saw Jesus at his baptism, God told him, *"The one you see the Spirit descending and resting on—he is the one who baptizes with the Holy Spirit."* (John 1:33) In the Old Testament, the Spirit came upon people temporarily and then left, but the Holy Spirit rested and remained on Jesus. This is why he can give the Spirit without measure. Jesus is the portal between heaven and earth, mediating the Spirit to all people who will receive him!

We often become threatened when we feel someone else might infringe on our ministry or our freedoms. John was the most revered Jew of his time but was not threatened when Jesus became more famous and drew larger crowds. In fact, this brought John incredible fulfillment, as he said, *"So this joy of mine is complete."*

Are you holding on too tightly to what God has entrusted to you? Are you willing to give it away as freely as you received it? Will you decrease so he can increase? This is the secret to complete joy.

REFLECT AND RESPOND

What is Jesus saying to me right now?

What step of faith is Jesus calling me to take today?

DAY 10

READ AND LISTEN: JOHN 4:1-26

Take a minute to listen for what God is saying in these verses…

COMMENT AND CONSIDER

Samaritans were the descendants of the northern ten tribes of Israel who intermarried with their Assyrian conquerors after 722 BC. Jews were the descendants of the two southern tribes who had not intermarried, which is the reason they considered Samaritans unclean apostates to be avoided whenever possible. Jacob's well, which is situated underground in a narrow valley between Mount Gerizim and Mount Ebal, near the modern Palestinian town of Nablus, still draws clear, cold water from over a hundred feet deep.

Ancient travelers in the Middle East typically walked about 20 miles a day and took a midday rest to avoid the heat of the day. As Jesus and his disciples approached Sychar, they decided to take a break at the ancient well Jacob had dug for his son Joseph. It was normal for village women to come in groups to draw water in the cool of the morning and evening, which often became an opportunity to socialize and catch up on the latest gossip. The fact that this Samaritan woman came to the well alone in the heat of the day may reflect her desire to avoid social contact.

It was not considered proper for a rabbi to engage with a woman in public who was not a part of his own extended family. Since Isaac, Jacob, and Moses all met their wives at wells, talking to a woman at a well was considered flirtatious. (See Genesis 24:12-17, 29:7-18, Exodus 2:16-21.) Even more scandalous was talking to a Samaritan woman, whom the rabbis automatically labeled an unclean heretic. This is why the woman was taken by surprise at Jesus' request for a drink. Then Jesus turned it around implying he had *"living water"* to offer her. Living water is flowing water rather than stagnant. He was not carrying the traditional leather bag with a folding frame that travelers often used to draw water from a well, so she couldn't imagine how he could give her a drink of any kind!

At this point Jesus clarified the living water he offered was something far more than a drink to temporarily quench her thirst. Instead, he was offering her the very source of life that would never stop providing what she needed most, *"a spring of water springing up in him for eternal life."* Perhaps Jesus had in mind the vision from Isaiah, *"You will joyfully draw water from the springs of salvation, and on that day you will say, 'Give thanks to the Lord; proclaim his name!'"* (Isaiah 12:3-4) Thinking he was offering her something like indoor plumbing, the woman asked Jesus to give it to her, so Jesus changed his approach and addressed the deepest needs his living water could satisfy.

The Spirit gave Jesus a prophetic insight into this woman's brokenness, things he could not have known on a simply human level. He perceived she had been divorced five times and was now living with a man outside of marriage. By asking her to go and call her husband, Jesus was gently bringing her pain and shame out into the open. Her ambiguous response, *"I have no husband"* could constitute an immoral proposition, given the questionable context of a single man addressing an unaccompanied woman at a well. But then Jesus delivered his prophetic insight about her string of broken marriages and current immoral living situation.

This painful revelation drove the woman to recognize Jesus' prophetic gifting, but she tried to change the subject by bringing up the religious controversy between Samaritans and Jews over worship on nearby Mount Gerizim versus worship on Mount Zion in Jerusalem. Jesus didn't allow her to sidetrack the conversation with these questions; instead, he pointed her back to the work of the Spirit transforming her life. Finally, she relented, admitting her longing for the long-awaited Prophet like Moses who would come to save her people. Jesus said plainly, *"I, the one speaking to you, am he."*

What brokenness in your life keeps you from being more open with Jesus and those around you? How can you open up despite that and allow Jesus to plant a spring of living water deeper into your heart?

REFLECT AND RESPOND

What is Jesus saying to me right now?

What step of faith is Jesus calling me to take today?

DAY 11

READ AND LISTEN: JOHN 4:27-42

Take a minute to listen for what God is saying in these verses…

COMMENT AND CONSIDER

Jesus sat down by Jacob's well, exhausted and hungry. By the time his disciples came back, he was energized and filled. A broken Samaritan woman came to Jacob's well by herself in the heat of the day to draw water with her clay jar. By the time she finished talking to Jesus she abandoned her water jar and ran back into the town of Sychar to tell everyone about the living water she had found! The disciples were shocked to come back and find Jesus talking by himself with a Samaritan woman who was a stranger but didn't question their Rabbi. They tried to strengthen him for their journey with food, but he told them, *"I have food to eat that you don't know about."*

Meanwhile the Samaritan woman of questionable reputation was talking to all the people in Sychar whom she previously tried to avoid. Men generally considered women unreliable witnesses, particularly women labeled immoral. But she kept telling them, *"Come, see a man who told me everything I ever did. Could this be the Messiah?"* The Samaritans did not believe in a Davidic Messiah but were awaiting the fulfilment of God's promise to Moses, *"I will raise up for them a prophet like you from among their brothers. I will put my words in his mouth, and he will tell them everything I command him."* (Deuteronomy 18:18)

Despite her compromised social position, the passion and conviction of this brave woman caught the attention of the people of Sychar. Living water already flowed from her life as she allowed the Holy Spirit to speak through her. Her testimony was so compelling that many overcame their judgmental prejudice and came out to see this man she had met. When the people heard Jesus for themselves, they wanted more of what he offered, so they invited him and his disciples to spend a couple days with them. Eventually, many of the people of Sychar came to believe in Jesus saying to the woman, *"We no longer believe because of what you said, since we have heard for ourselves and know that this really is the Savior of the world."*

Jesus explained to the disciples that mission is like farming. There is a time to plant and a time to harvest. In first-century Palestine, farmers typically planted barley in January and wheat in February. Approximately four months later, the grain was ready to be harvested. Ripe barley develops a plume which turns the fields white, a sure sign harvest time has come. Jesus sowed the Word in this Samaritan woman, and she was ready for harvest almost immediately. She, in turn, planted the seed of the Good News in her town, then Jesus and the disciples were able to help her bring in the harvest. The same people who plant do not always harvest, but we need to learn how to do both and recognize when the fields are white and ready.

Jesus demonstrated the *"person of peace"* missional principle he taught his disciples to follow. (See Luke 10:1-11.) He initiated the conversation with the Samaritan woman, and when he found her responsive, he invested in her life. She, in turn, did the same with the people of her town. She invited the ones who were open and responsive to come meet Jesus. He, in turn, spent time with them, and they ate meals together. Jesus was showing and telling them the Good News of the Kingdom until they also came to trust and receive him as their Lord and Savior. This is how we are to plant and harvest. This is how the Kingdom grows.

Have you met a man who told you everything you ever did? How motivated are you to tell others about him? What is your testimony of how he has changed your life? Do you know how to find and invest in people of peace? Are you ready to bring in the harvest? There is nothing more satisfying to a hungry soul!

REFLECT AND RESPOND

What is Jesus saying to me right now?

What step of faith is Jesus calling me to take today?

DAY 12

READ AND LISTEN: JOHN 4:43-54

Take a minute to listen for what God is saying in these verses…

COMMENT AND CONSIDER

While Jesus was in Cana, a *"royal official"* came to him from Capernaum with a desperate plea to heal his dying son. Although Herod Antipas, son of Herod the Great and Tetrarch of Galilee, lacked the royal title "King" like his father, this official was probably part of Antipas' court. Luke tells us one of Jesus' key female disciples was *Joanna the wife of Chuza, Herod's steward,* a member of Antipas' government. (Luke 8:3) We don't know if this is the same family, but if not, they certainly knew each other. Antipas' new capital of Tiberias was the seat of his government, and this official lived relatively nearby in Capernaum on the north shore of the Sea of Galilee, the town Jesus had adopted as his new hometown. John tells us this healing story is *"the second sign Jesus performed."*

John weaves seven miracles throughout his narrative of Jesus' life, each one a *"sign"* meant to reveal Jesus' true identity and plant faith in the hearts of those who read about them. He explained his purpose in writing near the end of the Gospel: *Jesus performed many other signs in the presence of his disciples that are not written in this book. But these are written so that you may believe that Jesus is the Messiah, the Son of God, and that by believing you may have life in his name.* (John 20:30-31) The seven signs are: changing water into wine at the wedding at Cana (2:1-11), healing the royal official's son in Capernaum (4:46-54), healing the paralyzed man at the pool of Bethesda in Jerusalem (5:1-15), feeding the 5,000 at the Sea of Galilee (6:5-14), walking on water in the Sea of Galilee (6:16-21), healing the man born blind in the pool of Siloam in Jerusalem (9:1-7), and raising Lazarus from the dead in Bethany (11:1-45).

Although John offers these signs to help us believe, Jesus is sometimes critical of those who continually demand more signs yet fail to believe. During the Exodus God tired of the Israelites failing to trust him despite all the miracles he performed. *The Lord said to Moses, "How long will these people despise me? How long will they not trust in me despite all the signs I have performed among them?"* (Numbers 14:11) When the Pharisees demanded more miracles to test him, Jesus was equally frustrated. *Sighing deeply in his spirit, he said, "Why does this generation demand a sign? Truly I tell you, no sign will be given to this generation."* (Mark 8:12)

So how are we to understand Jesus' response to the royal official when he asked Jesus to come and heal his son, *"Unless you people see signs and wonders, you will not believe"*? Was he criticizing the official for demanding a sign or was he affirming the role of signs to help him believe? When Jesus pushed back on his request, the man pleaded again for his son's life, and Jesus saw he was coming in genuine desperation, asking for the help only he could give. This is how the signs of John's Gospel are meant to function, to help those who are genuinely seeking faith to put their trust more fully in Jesus.

In this case, Jesus stretched the royal official's faith further by declaring the boy's healing from over 20 miles away. The man chose to believe Jesus and returned from Cana down to Capernaum. While he was still traveling the following day, his servants met him on the road with the joyful news of his son's recovery. Further inquiry revealed the boy was healed at the very hour Jesus declared him well!

What helps you trust Jesus more fully? Have you seen miraculous signs which have helped you to believe? When is it not appropriate to ask Jesus for a miracle?

REFLECT AND RESPOND

What is Jesus saying to me right now?

What step of faith is Jesus calling me to take today?

FOOTSTEPS EVERY WEEK: REVIEW

Write a brief summary of what Jesus said to you each day this past week and the step of faith he called you to take:

MONDAY

TUESDAY

WEDNESDAY

THURSDAY

FRIDAY

SATURDAY

FOOTSTEPS EVERY WEEK: REFLECT

BIG PICTURE

As you look over what Jesus has said to you this past week, do you see any themes? What is the most important thing you need to remember and believe?

PREDICTABLE PATTERN

As you look over what Jesus called you to do this past week, is there a new predictable pattern he is inviting you to establish in your life with God and others?

PLANT THE WORD

As you look over the readings from this past week, write out the passage that feels most important for you and memorize it over the next week:

DAY 13

READ AND LISTEN: JOHN 5:1-16

COMMENT AND CONSIDER

Since Jerusalem only had one natural water source, the Gihon Spring in the Kidron Valley, Herod the Great built a massive water system bringing water from springs many miles away. The water first filled three enormous pools south of Bethlehem, with a total capacity of 75 million gallons. From there two aqueducts brought the water to a series of pools in Jerusalem, including the Pools of Bethesda. Centuries earlier the small valley north of the Temple had been dammed to create a reservoir to collect rainwater. This was eventually expanded into two large pools, about 40 feet deep and separated by the dam. They came to be called the Pools of Bethesda, meaning "house of mercy."

John gives a detailed description of these pools, *By the Sheep Gate in Jerusalem there is a pool, called Bethesda in Aramaic, which has five colonnades.* Critical scholars questioned the historical accuracy of his description because there were no examples of five-sided pools with colonnades that had ever been discovered. But when archaeologists excavated the pools, they discovered continuous colonnades running along all four sides of the pools, plus a colonnade running across the dam separating them, totaling five porticoes. They also discovered immediately next to the huge water storage pools a pagan healing shrine dedicated to the Greek god of healing, Asclepius.

Shrines to Asclepius were very popular in the Roman Empire. The nearby Antonia Fortress would have supplied plenty of customers in the form of Roman soldiers looking for cures to their ailments. When someone seeking healing came to an Asclepion, they made an offering to the god, shared a special meal with the priests, took a bath in a small pool, received a hallucinogenic drink, and then fell into a deep sleep in one of the dark caves or rooms provided. They believed Asclepius would come to them in their drug-induced dreams to heal them. In fact, the priests often performed medical procedures on their anesthetized patients, sometimes resulting in genuine improvements.

This explains why *a large number of the disabled—blind, lame, and paralyzed* lay in the porticoes around the pools. However, they did not look to the huge water storage pools for healing, but rather the small pools and caves of the healing shrine. Jesus intentionally went to this group of desperate and suffering people during his visit to Jerusalem for one of the great festivals. He approached one particularly hopeless man who had paralyzed for 38 years and asked him *"Do you want to get well?"* This seems a strange question to ask a man who is laying on his mat next to a healing shrine! But Jesus perceived his physical disability had become an excuse for living a miserable existence. The man could not even answer Jesus' question directly, instead complaining about why he was destined to remain in his paralyzed state.

Normally, when Jesus healed people, he affirmed them for the role their faith played in their healing. (See Matthew 9:22 for one example.) However, this man had no apparent faith, didn't know who Jesus was, and wouldn't even express a desire for healing. Jesus healed him anyway saying, *"Get up, pick up your mat and walk,"* and the man stood up for the first time in 38 years!

It happened to be a Sabbath day, so immediately the religious leaders zeroed in on the fact Jesus told him to carry his mat, violating their interpretation of the Sabbath laws. But the healed paralytic couldn't identify his healer until Jesus met him later in the nearby Temple courts. The man still did not express any faith or even appreciation for what Jesus had done for him. Instead, he went immediately to the religious authorities and informed on Jesus, resulting in intensified persecution of Jesus by the religious leaders.

Do you ever intentionally spend time with hurting people? Do you think it is possible to become too comfortable in your brokenness? Do you ever fail to recognize Jesus as the source of blessing in your life? How will you respond to him right now?

REFLECT AND RESPOND

What is Jesus saying to me right now?

What step of faith is Jesus calling me to take today?

DAY 14

READ AND LISTEN: JOHN 5:17-30

Take a minute to listen for what God is saying in these verses…

COMMENT AND CONSIDER

The Jews were the only people in the ancient world to set aside an entire 24-hour period each week as a time of rest and restoration. In the surrounding pagan cultures, people simply worked day after day, week after week, with no break except for the occasional religious feast or festival. This pattern of weekly rest was woven into the biblical account of God's six days of creative work, followed by rest on the seventh day. Over time this distinctive rhythm took on increasingly greater significance in Judaism. Eventually, the rabbis added more layers of ritual and restriction to protect the sanctity of the Sabbath day. They saw this as planting a "hedge" around the Law to ensure no one could even get close to breaking it.

At the time of Jesus, these extra-biblical rules about what you could and could not do on the seventh day were passed down orally from one generation of rabbis to the next and were only written down in the Mishnah around AD 200. The Pharisees were very enthusiastic about these extra rules and rituals, but Jesus was not. In fact, he often came into conflict with the Pharisees because he openly flouted their religious practices. He was faithful to the written Law of the Old Testament, saying, *"Don't think that I came to abolish the Law or the Prophets"* (Matthew 5:17), but he rejected the rules and rituals the Pharisees added to the Law, particularly when they contradicted the intent of the Law. He said to them, *"You have a fine way of invalidating God's command in order to set up your tradition!"* (Mark 7:9)

Jesus' healing activity on the Sabbath most often brought him into conflict with the religious leaders. The rabbis ruled that only matters of life and death were to be addressed on the Sabbath. Anything that could be postponed to the other days of the week should be done then. Jesus had a different perspective. Responding to the criticism of his healing the paralyzed man, Jesus said, *"My Father is still working, and I am working also."*

The rabbis recognized God did not cease from all activity on the Sabbath; otherwise the universe would cease to exist! Philo, the first-century Jewish philosopher from Alexandria, said that God sustained the universe on the Sabbath day, but it required no labor because it is God's very nature that sustains all things.

Jesus said something very similar about his healing ministry. He explained his absolute dependence on the Father and that his life simply flowed from the example of his Father. *"Truly I tell you, the Son is not able to do anything on his own, but only what he sees the Father doing. For whatever the Father does, the Son likewise does these things."* If the Father was doing it, then Jesus was doing it. He said something similar about his teaching ministry, *"So the things that I speak, I speak just as the Father has told me."* (John 12:50) This was the secret of Jesus' extraordinary life!

Following the Way of Jesus is learning to hear what God is saying and see what God is doing so we can do and say likewise. Jesus is the one who shows us what the Father is doing and tells us what the Father is saying. As he said, *"anyone who hears my word and believes him who sent me has eternal life and will not come under judgment but has passed from death to life."* When Jesus described himself as the Good Shepherd, he said, *"The sheep follow him because they know his voice."* (John 10:4) Jesus' disciples will learn to hear what he is saying and see what he is doing so they can follow him, even if it does not fit the assumptions of human rituals and religion.

How is human religion keeping you from doing the things Jesus did? Is your life flowing from the life of Jesus? How can you learn to hear the voice of your Shepherd more clearly so you can follow him more closely?

REFLECT AND RESPOND

What is Jesus saying to me right now?

What step of faith is Jesus calling me to take today?

DAY 15

READ AND LISTEN: JOHN 5:31-47

Take a minute to listen for what God is saying in these verses…

COMMENT AND CONSIDER

In the first century, many Jewish messianic pretenders gathered enthusiastic followers, made grandiose claims, took up arms against Rome, and were quickly crushed. Jesus was careful not to make overt messianic claims too early in his ministry, because he didn't want the authorities to shut him down before he could accomplish all he was sent to do. Even when he affirmed his true identity to his inner circle, *he gave the disciples orders to tell no one that he was the Messiah.* (Matthew 16:20)

Despite this careful balance of self-disclosure, Jesus was very direct in calling people to believe in him. (See John 11:26, 14:2.) But on what basis are we to distinguish Jesus from messianic pretenders so we can confidently put our trust in him? Jesus admitted self-testimony is not enough because anyone can make any claim they want about themselves. He said, *"If I testify about myself, my testimony is not true."* Instead, Jesus offered four trustworthy sources that testify to the truth of his messianic mission and identity. First, he pointed to his cousin John the Baptist saying, *"You sent messengers to John, and he testified to the truth."* John was certainly the most revered Jew of his time and drew huge crowds who admired his courageous message and the integrity of his lifestyle. John consistently pointed to Jesus as the Messiah for whom he was preparing the way. As Jesus said, *"John was a burning and shining lamp, and you were willing to rejoice for a while in his light."*

Secondly, Jesus pointed to the example of his way of life and the miracles he performed as a powerful testimony to his identity and the truth of his claims. *"These very works I am doing testify about me that the Father has sent me."* Jesus consistently demonstrated he was motivated by love for all people by welcoming the outcast, lifting up the lowly, and offering forgiveness to sinners. In addition, he demonstrated supernatural compassion by healing the broken, liberating the oppressed, and raising the dead. Jesus said, *"If I am not doing my Father's works, don't believe me. But if I am doing them and you don't believe me, believe the works. This way you will know and understand that the Father is in me and I in the Father." (John 10:37-38)*

The third testimony to the truth of Jesus is his own heavenly Father. *"The Father who sent me has himself testified about me."* At Jesus' baptism the heavens were torn open, the Holy Spirit was poured out and the Father spoke from heaven, *"You are my beloved Son; with you I am well-pleased."* (Mark 1:11) When he took his closest disciples on a mountain retreat, Jesus' appearance was transfigured, and the Father spoke from heaven, *"This is my beloved Son; listen to him!"* (Mark 9:7)

The fourth testimony to Jesus is the Word of God. Jesus said, *"You pore over the Scriptures because you think you have eternal life in them, and yet they testify about me."* The messianic prophecies woven throughout the Old Testament are fulfilled beautifully in Jesus. Moses, the most important biblical figure in first-century Judaism, was traditionally identified as the author of the Pentateuch, the most important books of the Bible. Jesus said, *"For if you believed Moses, you would believe me, because he wrote about me. But if you don't believe what he wrote, how will you believe my words?"*

Despite these powerful confirming testimonies, many people still refused to believe in Jesus. They were quick to believe revolutionary figures who simply made messianic claims with nothing to back up those claims. The same is true today. Jesus' identity as the Son of God was conclusively demonstrated by John the Baptist's prophecies, the consistent example of Jesus' extraordinary way of life, his fulfilment of Scripture, and the direct revelation of God the Father.

How do these testimonies strengthen your faith in Jesus and your resolve to follow him? Are you prepared to share these testimonies along with your own personal story so that others will come to believe?

REFLECT AND RESPOND

What is Jesus saying to me right now?

What step of faith is Jesus calling me to take today?

DAY 16

READ AND LISTEN: JOHN 6:1-15

Take a minute to listen for what God is saying in these verses…

COMMENT AND CONSIDER

Jesus' feeding of the 5,000 is the only miracle recorded in all four Gospels. Matthew and Mark record two miraculous feedings, one with 5,000 people on the western shore and another with 4,000 people on the eastern shore. Luke and John only tell us of a feeding of 5,000, and John specifies that number does not include the women and children who were present. John is less clear about the location, but offers the detail, *There was plenty of grass in that place,* which sounds like the traditional location of Tabgha, just west of Capernaum, a place of seven natural springs that is very cool and lush still today. This fits the context of the Synoptic accounts which explain this miracle took place when Jesus and the disciples had retreated for a time of rest but were found by the crowds. John hints at a time away with the disciples when he writes, *"Jesus went up a mountain and sat down there with his disciples."* Again, this sounds like a retreat at Tabgha. However, in the next passage John tells us they *rowed about three or four miles* on their way to Capernaum before they encountered Jesus walking on the water. (John 6:19) Capernaum is less than two miles east of Tabgha. Did the wind blow them off course? We are left with lingering questions about the exact location of the miracle.

After Jesus taught the huge crowd all day, a crisis loomed as they realized there was not enough food in that remote spot to feed the hungry people listening to him. Going to buy bread for a crowd that size was impractical, costing more than half a year's wages. John makes explicit what the other Gospel writers imply, that Jesus wanted to use this as a teaching moment for his disciples. By asking Philip how they would feed such a crowd, Jesus challenged them to face their inability to meet the need confronting them. Andrew sheepishly offered the only food they could find, *"There's a boy here who has five barley loaves and two fish—but what are they for so many?"* As he pointed out, five loaves and two fish was a ridiculously insufficient meal for 5,000-15,000 people, and it wasn't even theirs!

Once the disciples were fully aware of their inability to meet this need, Jesus taught them how to overcome the challenge of insufficient resources. He had them organize the people in in groups on the grass, then took the bread and fish, praying the traditional thanksgiving prayer over them: *Baruch atah Adonai, Eloheinu melech haolam…* "Blessed are you Lord our God, King of the universe…" The Synoptics tell us Jesus divided the bread and fish between his twelve disciples and sent them to feed the people. What a learning experience that must have been! It took an exercise of faith to wade into a crowd of hungry people with less than half a loaf and one sixth of a fish to feed thousands of hungry people. And then they experienced the miracle first-hand. Imagine watching the bread and fish grow rather than diminish while person after person took what they needed to satisfy their hunger. When the whole crowd had eaten their fill, the disciples gathered the leftover pieces of the barley loaves—enough to fill twelve baskets!

It wasn't just the disciples who were moved by this miraculous feeding. The people who ate their fill saw there was no human way that little boy's lunch could ever have fed even a fraction of the people gathered there. The realization rippled through the crowd that the one who could feed thousands with five loaves and two fish must be their long-awaited king, descended from David and foretold by the Prophets. As the people started to surge toward Jesus, he slipped away into the crowd, much as he did in Nazareth when the crowd wanted to stone him. (See Luke 4:30.) Jesus was their long-awaited King, but his rule would be established in a very different way than they expected—not in Herod's Palace, but on a Roman cross.

Do you ever feel inadequate for the things God has called you to do? Are you willing to wade into the crowd by faith like the disciples did and trust God to provide?

REFLECT AND RESPOND

What is Jesus saying to me right now?

What step of faith is Jesus calling me to take today?

DAY 17

READ AND LISTEN: JOHN 6:16-24

Take a minute to listen for what God is saying in these verses…

COMMENT AND CONSIDER

Jesus had withdrawn from the crowds who were about to forcibly pressure him to lead a rebellion against Rome. He also took the opportunity for some precious time alone. The desolate, basalt-strewn hillsides overlooking the north shore of the Sea of Galilee was a favorite area for Jesus when he needed to get away from people and spend some intentional time with his Father. (See Luke 5:16.) Jesus instructed the disciples to return home without him, so they got into their boat and pushed out from shore. (See Mark 6:45.) Although night was falling, four of the disciples were seasoned fishermen who regularly plied their trade at night and thus were very accustomed to sailing in the dark.

The Sea of Galilee is a beautiful freshwater lake that sits in a deep depression of the Jordan Rift Valley, some 700 feet below sea level. It is subject to unpredictable weather events. The storm John describes here was not as violent as the one that was sinking their boats while Jesus slept peacefully in the stern (compare Mark 4:37-38), but strong winds from the east blew against them and powerful waves battered the boat. Straining against the oars, they were blown off course, not able to make headway in the direction of Capernaum. By now they were far from land and had no choice except to keep rowing. Just as dawn broke, they saw a figure out on the water. They were afraid because they knew it was impossible for a man to walk on water without sinking. They assumed it must be a ghost! (See Mark 6:49.) Many first-century Jews believed in night spirits or the spirits of drowning victims who would appear at sea. These stories were particularly popular with sailors and fishermen.

Jesus reassured them by identifying himself, *"It is I. Don't be afraid."* Realizing who it was, they brought him aboard, and as soon as Jesus got into the boat with them the wind ceased and suddenly they arrived at Capernaum. The disciples knew Jesus was a real human being because they spent day after day with him, engaging in all the normal human activities that are common to everyone everywhere: eating, drinking, sleeping, talking, sweating, laughing, crying. But they knew he was also so much more. Job tells us God is the only one who walks on water, *"He alone stretches out the heavens and treads on the waves of the sea."* (Job 9:8) Jesus' statement *"It is I"* can also be translated *"I am,"* the statement of absolute being reserved for God in the Bible. (See Exodus 3:14.) Matthew tells us their reaction was to worship him, declaring "Truly you are the Son of God." (Matthew 14:33)

This miracle is the fifth of the seven *"signs"* John incorporates into his narrative. Turning water into wine, feeding the 5,000, and walking on water are the signs that point to Jesus' authority over the physical laws of the universe. He is not bound to obey the laws of nature; on the contrary, they must obey his command. Likewise, his healing of the royal official's son, his healing of the paralyzed man at the Pools of Bethesda, and soon his restoration of sight to the man born blind at the Pool of Siloam demonstrate his compassion and authority over the natural laws of the human body. The final of these seven signs, the raising of Lazarus after four days in the tomb, demonstrates Jesus' authority over life and death, leaving no doubt as to his true identity, the divine Son of God and Messianic King!

When the wind is against you and you are straining against the oars, how quick are you to welcome Jesus into your boat? When the laws of the universe seem to be against you, do you recognize Jesus' divine authority over all things? Do you recognize the signs Jesus is showing you today?

REFLECT AND RESPOND

What is Jesus saying to me right now?

What step of faith is Jesus calling me to take today?

DAY 18

Read and Listen: John 6:25-40

Take a minute to listen for what God is saying in these verses…

Comment and Consider

Many Jews in Jesus' time were waiting for God to fulfill his promise to send a great Prophet like Moses to lead his people out of bondage and into the promised land of freedom from Rome. God promised Moses, *"I will raise up for them a prophet like you from among their brothers. I will put my words in his mouth, and he will tell them everything I command him."* (Deuteronomy 18:18) When Jesus fed the 5,000 with five barley loaves and two fish, it ignited the hope that Jesus was that Prophet like Moses, finally come to lead his people out of slavery to the Gentiles, which is why they wanted to force him to become king. (See John 6:15.)

When the crowds, who had withdrawn to Herod Antipas' capital of Tiberias for the night, returned to the place of the miraculous feeding, they couldn't find Jesus and the disciples. So naturally they went to Jesus' new hometown of Capernaum and found them there. There must have been too many people to fit into the extended family home of Simon and Andrew where they normally met, so instead they gathered in the large synagogue just one block north of the house. (See John 6:59.) Synagogues served as community centers for public gatherings and discourse, in addition to the weekly Sabbath gatherings for teaching and prayer. Archaeologists have found the foundations of the actual synagogue in Capernaum where this took place.

One of the popular first-century beliefs about the Prophet like Moses was that he would supply daily manna for the people as God did for the Israelites in the wilderness and they would no longer have to work for food. Jesus' miraculous feeding reinforced that expectation. It didn't take Jesus long to discern this was the reason these people were pursuing him. He said, *"Truly I tell you, you are looking for me, not because you saw the signs, but because you ate the loaves and were filled."* Jesus warned them not to seek after the food which quickly passes away, but to seek a relationship with him which would feed their deepest hungers and satisfy them forever.

Thinking Jesus wanted them to do something in order for him to perform another meal miracle, they asked, *"What can we do to perform the works of God?"* Again, Jesus tried to point them toward a relationship with him. He replied, *"This is the work of God—that you believe in the one he has sent."* They still didn't understand the relational invitation Jesus was offering. Finally, they came out and said exactly what they wanted from him, *"What are you going to perform? Our ancestors ate the manna in the wilderness, just as it is written: He gave them bread from heaven to eat."*

Picking up on the language of their quote from Exodus 16:4, Jesus clarified *bread from heaven* is not the manna that fell from the sky, but rather *"the one who comes down from heaven and gives life to the world."* Still thinking Jesus was offering to give them physical bread from heaven, they said excitedly, *"Sir, give us this bread always."* Jesus made it as clear as he could with the first of his seven great I AM statements in John's Gospel: *"I am the bread of life."* Jesus went on to explain that coming to him and believing in him was the only way to receive this heavenly bread that alone can fill the emptiness in the human soul and satisfy the longing of the human heart. He even went so far as to explain the outcome of a relationship with him is a life that triumphs over death; *"For this is the will of my Father: that everyone who sees the Son and believes in him will have eternal life, and I will raise him up on the last day."*

What draws you to Jesus? Is what you are seeking aligned with what he is offering? How can you learn to receive the true bread from heaven that alone will satisfy your deepest longings and fill you with his life?

REFLECT AND RESPOND

What is Jesus saying to me right now?

What step of faith is Jesus calling me to take today?

FOOTSTEPS EVERY WEEK: REVIEW

Write a brief summary of what Jesus said to you each day this past week and the step of faith he called you to take:

MONDAY

TUESDAY

WEDNESDAY

THURSDAY

FRIDAY

SATURDAY

Footsteps Every Week: Reflect

Big Picture
As you look over what Jesus has said to you this past week, do you see any themes? What is the most important thing you need to remember and believe?

Predictable Pattern
As you look over what Jesus called you to do this past week, is there a new predictable pattern he is inviting you to establish in your life with God and others?

Plant the Word
As you look over the readings from this past week, write out the passage that feels most important for you and memorize it over the next week:

DAY 19

READ AND LISTEN: JOHN 6:41-59

Take a minute to listen for what God is saying in these verses…

COMMENT AND CONSIDER

When God appeared to Moses in the burning bush and called him to set his people free from slavery, Moses asked him, *"If I go to the Israelites and say to them, 'The God of your ancestors has sent me to you,' and they ask me, 'What is his name?' what should I tell them?"* God replied to Moses, *"I AM WHO I AM."* (Exodus 3:13-14) This personal name that God revealed to Moses is comprised of four Hebrew consonants YHWH, called the "tetragrammaton," meaning "the four letters." Usually transliterated into English as *"Yahweh,"* the divine name is often represented in English translations of the Bible as *Lord* in small capitals.

These four Hebrew consonants form the root word for being. It can be translated many different ways, including "I am who I am," "I am what I am," "I will be who I will be," "I will be who I am," etc. The meaning of this name is that God is the ground of all being who exists independent of anyone or anything else, the one on whom everyone and everything depends for its very existence. It is usually translated simply as "I AM." The rabbis came to believe this personal name of God was so holy that it should not be spoken out loud, so when reading out loud passages containing the name Yahweh they began to substitute the Hebrew word *"Adonai,"* which means "Lord."

When Jesus said, *"I am the bread of life"* and *"the one who comes down from heaven"* he was using theologically loaded language that amounted to a provocative claim of divinity. This is why the crowd began grumbling, *"Isn't this Jesus the son of Joseph, whose father and mother we know? How can he now say, 'I have come down from heaven'?"* After all, Jesus was born in Bethlehem, grew up in Nazareth, and had parents, brothers and sisters. How could he be divine? Admitting that this is a mystery difficult to understand, Jesus pointed out that only the work of the Spirit in the willing hearts of those who receive his word will be able to believe. *"No one can come to me unless the Father who sent me draws him, and I will raise him up on the last day."* Then Jesus quoted Isaiah 54:13, *"It is written in the Prophets: And they will all be taught by God."*

Are we willing to listen and learn from Jesus, or will we allow our presuppositions to keep us from receiving the truth about him? Pointing ahead to his death on the cross, Jesus reiterated the nature and means of the promise: *"I am the living bread that came down from heaven. If anyone eats of this bread he will live forever. The bread that I will give for the life of the world is my flesh."* When the people heard him equate the bread of heaven with his flesh, it sounded like cannibalism to them. But instead of softening the controversy, Jesus pressed into the scandal of his coming crucifixion, *"Truly I tell you, unless you eat the flesh of the Son of Man and drink his blood, you do not have life in yourselves."*

From the perspective of those who live after Jesus' death and resurrection, we see the profound truth that Jesus is the Lamb of God who takes away the sin of the world. In the Lord's Supper, we eat bread and drink wine which Jesus reinterpreted from the Passover meal as his own body and blood, broken and shed on the cross for the forgiveness of the sins of the world. But to these people who wanted Jesus on their own terms, it just sounded like blasphemy.

Do you err on the side of underestimating Jesus' full divinity or full humanity? How can Jesus' statement *"I am the bread of life"* challenge your presuppositions and enrich your relationship with Jesus? Are you willing to receive and trust Jesus' words even when you can't fully understand them?

REFLECT AND RESPOND

What is Jesus saying to me right now?

What step of faith is Jesus calling me to take today?

DAY 20

READ AND LISTEN: JOHN 6:60-71

Take a minute to listen for what God is saying in these verses…

COMMENT AND CONSIDER

As Jesus began preaching in synagogues and healing the sick, his fame grew almost instantly. The Jewish people had been oppressed for centuries, and the longing for a deliverer had reached a fever pitch. People were amazed at Jesus' authority when they heard him speak as a direct representative of his heavenly Father. They saw him demonstrate the Kingdom by doing God's will on earth as it is done in heaven. Before long the towns of Galilee couldn't contain the crowds who flocked to Jesus, so they had to gather on the open hillsides and in the massive Temple courts. However, Jesus didn't seem to care about this kind of fame and popularity. He treated the outcast and sinners as more important than people of influence. He said and did things that were controversial and didn't endear himself to those with social and political power. He called tax collectors, welcomed prostitutes, and embraced lepers.

Jesus sometimes told confusing parables, like the story praising a dishonest steward. (See Luke 16:1-8.) He said things that were unpopular such as *"whoever doesn't take up his cross and follow me is not worthy of me. Anyone who finds his life will lose it, and anyone who loses his life because of me will find it."* (Matthew 10:38-39) But one of the most controversial things Jesus ever said was, *"Truly I tell you, unless you eat the flesh of the Son of Man and drink his blood, you do not have life in yourselves.* (John 6:53) Drinking the blood of animals was strictly forbidden (Leviticus 17:10-12) and eating human flesh was unthinkable to a righteous Jew. It is hard to imagine a more challenging statement than this!

In hindsight we understand Jesus was pointing to his institution of the Lord's Supper in which we eat the bread and drink the wine as a way of communing with Jesus and each other in a sacred covenantal meal. But even to his own disciples, these words seemed incomprehensible and unacceptable. As they said, *"This teaching is hard. Who can accept it?"* Jesus did not respond by softening his words or explaining them; instead, he took it to another level of challenge when he said, *"Does this offend you? Then what if you were to observe the Son of Man ascending to where he was before?"* This seeming call to cannibalism and reference to his bodily ascension was too much for even his extended circle of disciples to accept. Not only did the crowds disappear, but John says, *From that moment many of his disciples turned back and no longer accompanied him.*

What was Jesus doing? He recognized a consumeristic culture growing up around his miracles and saw that many were following him for the wrong reasons. Jesus was giving incredibly high challenge to weed out those who were simply there for what they could get from Jesus from those who were ready to trust him enough to submit and follow, even if they didn't fully understand. He was using high challenge to prune the crowds and test the people to see who was ready to become an actual disciple who submits. More is not always better. Jesus is not looking for more fans; he is calling committed followers.

It was a poignant moment when Jesus turned to his inner circle of full-time disciples and asked them, *"You don't want to go away too, do you?"* At that point they could have chosen to go their own way and return to their regular day jobs. But Peter, recognizing the unique opportunity Jesus offered, said, *"Lord, to whom will we go? You have the words of eternal life."* The twelve disciples chose to trust Jesus even when they didn't understand. They decided to submit and follow Jesus no matter what. They determined not just to be fans of Jesus, but to take up their cross, leave everything else behind and follow him.

What things that Jesus said and did are hard for you to understand or accept? How is Jesus calling you to trust him and submit to his leading even if you don't understand? Are you a fan of Jesus or one of his followers?

REFLECT AND RESPOND

What is Jesus saying to me right now?

What step of faith is Jesus calling me to take today?

DAY 21

Read and Listen: John 7:1-13

Take a minute to listen for what God is saying in these verses…

Comment and Consider

Jesus lived his whole life under the ominous shadow of those who wanted him dead. When he was still a baby, Herod the Great plotted to murder the newborn King. (Matthew 2:13) Joseph and Mary returned to Nazareth to distance themselves from Herod's murderous son Archelaus, but still had to live under the rule of his other son Antipas who eventually sought to kill Jesus. (See Matthew 2:22 and Luke 13:31.) When Jesus cast his vision of the Messianic Kingdom for all people in Nazareth, the townspeople tried to stone him to death. (See Luke 4:28-29.) Early in Jesus' Galilean mission, the Pharisees plotted with the Herodians to kill him. (See Mark 3:6.) From the time Jesus healed the man at the Pools of Bethesda, the religious leaders in Jerusalem never stopped discussing how to put him to death. (See John 5:18.)

Jesus was fully aware of the opposition he faced and the dangers it posed. He knew his ultimate destiny was to go to Jerusalem and be executed, but he also knew the Father had specific things for him to accomplish first. Jesus was very careful not to reveal his identity too soon lest he be arrested and killed before he could complete his work. That is why he so often ordered those he healed to tell no one. (See Mark 7:36.)

In chapter 7 John tells us how, at this stage in his mission, Jesus returned to north Galilee, because the threat from the authorities had grown too dangerous in Judea. Eventually he came home to Nazareth. Jesus' mother and siblings were among those who did not believe in him. They did not stand with Jesus or defend him when the people of Nazareth tried to kill him at the beginning of his public ministry. When they heard reports of the things he was saying and doing, they thought he had gone crazy and went to Capernaum to bring him back home to Nazareth. (See Mark 3:21, 31-35.) John tells us directly *not even his brothers believed in him.*

When Jesus came home, his brothers told him he should return to Jerusalem and openly attend the Festival of Shelters, one of the three great Jewish holidays also known as Tabernacles or Booths. During this eight-day celebration, Jewish men slept in simple shelters built on the rooftops or in the courtyards of their homes to remember the years the children of Israel wandered through the Sinai desert. It is hard to know if Jesus' brothers had heard reports of those who were plotting to kill him, but it seems clear they were cynically baiting Jesus when they told him he should openly reveal himself at the Festival.

Jesus responded by telling them *"My time has not yet arrived, but your time is always at hand."* He was not going to the festival openly because it was not time for him to be arrested yet, but it was always time for them to repent and put their trust in him. Eventually his brothers became his followers like their mother Mary, but it took him rising from the dead to shake them from their spiritual blindness. The brothers did travel to Jerusalem for the Festival, presumably with their extended family. (See Luke 2:41.) Jesus went later, but wisely chose to keep his presence a secret so he could avoid the authorities and choose the right moment to begin teaching in the Temple courts.

Jesus never flinched from confronting those who opposed his Father's will and stood in the way of the Kingdom of God. He was not afraid to arouse violent opposition by speaking the truth, but he was also guided by his sense of destiny, deeply aware of the Father's calling and purpose for his life. He was determined to complete his mission by discerning his Father's timing without shying away from the sacrifice it would ultimately require.

Do you have a sense of God's purpose for your life? Are you seeking to fulfill your divine destiny according to God's timing? Are you prepared to pay the price it will cost you to complete your mission? How can Jesus' example help you find your way?

REFLECT AND RESPOND

What is Jesus saying to me right now?

What step of faith is Jesus calling me to take today?

DAY 22

READ AND LISTEN: JOHN 7:14-24

Take a minute to listen for what God is saying in these verses…

COMMENT AND CONSIDER

From about the age of five to twelve, Jewish boys typically attended primary school, called *Beth Sefer* (Hebrew for "house of the book) in the synagogue where the rabbis taught them to read and recite the Law. At about the age of twelve, these boys completed their education and began their apprenticeship into the family business. The best students could apply for secondary education, called *Beth Midrash* (Hebrew for "house of interpretation"), where they would memorize and debate the rabbinical rulings. This Oral Law was not written down but was passed down from generation to generation by memory. At around the age of eighteen, young men who studied in *Beth Midrash* could serve as scribes who copied manuscripts and composed legal documents. The best of those students could apply to become a disciple of the rabbi, called *Beth Talmid* (Hebrew for "house of learning"). They lived with the rabbi and his extended family, listening to everything he said and watching everything he did. At about the age of thirty, these disciples could be recognized as rabbis in their own right, and they then began training their own disciples.

While Jesus probably attended *Beth Sefer* as a boy, he did not receive secondary education or advanced training to be formally recognized as a rabbi. The people of Nazareth described Jesus as *"the carpenter."* (Mark 6:3) The Greek word *tekton* translated *"carpenter"* here is better translated "builder." This means Jesus apprenticed with his father and uncles to become a stonemason in the family building business. When the people of Nazareth heard Jesus teaching in the synagogue, they asked, *"Where did this man get this wisdom and these miraculous powers? Isn't this the carpenter's son? … So where does he get all these things?"* (Matthew 13:54-56)

About halfway through the eight-day Festival of Shelters, Jesus discerned he could begin teaching publicly without getting arrested, so he stepped forward in one of the great stone porticoes that surrounded the Temple courts and began teaching the crowds who had gathered to listen to the best teachers in Israel. As usual, the people were amazed at the authority and insight of Jesus' teaching, which could not be explained by his level of education. They said, *"How is this man so learned, since he hasn't been trained?"*

Jesus explained the source of his powerful teaching: *"My teaching isn't mine but is from the one who sent me."* Formally trained rabbis taught by quoting the rulings of other rabbis who had gone before them. Their teaching was a derivative message based on the interpretations they had received from their rabbis, who in turn had received them from other rabbis. By contrast Jesus spoke as a direct representative of his heavenly Father, claiming direct revelation. As he said, *"So the things that I speak, I speak just as the Father has told me."* (John 12:50)

The people debated this question—is Jesus' teaching really from God? Before Jesus even began speaking, they were already arguing about this. *Some were saying, "He's a good man." Others were saying, "No, on the contrary, he's deceiving the people."* (John 7:12) Once he began teaching, the debate intensified. Jesus said the religious leaders wanted to kill him for healing on the Sabbath (see John 5:18) but pointed out their hypocrisy because they freely performed circumcisions on the Sabbath. The crowd accused Jesus of paranoia, *"You have a demon!... Who is trying to kill you?"*

In the midst of this debate, Jesus offered a simple way to discern whether his teaching is from God: *"If anyone wants to do his will, he will know whether the teaching is from God or whether I am speaking on my own."* Jesus went on to say those who seek their own glory are serving themselves, but those who are seeking to glorify God speak on his behalf.

How do you discern the truth of Jesus' teaching? If Jesus' teaching really is a direct revelation from God, what are the implications for your life? Are you truly submitted to Jesus' teaching even when it challenges you, or do you try to make it fit your own agenda?

REFLECT AND RESPOND

What is Jesus saying to me right now?

What step of faith is Jesus calling me to take today?

DAY 23

READ AND LISTEN: JOHN 7:25-36

Take a minute to listen for what God is saying in these verses…

COMMENT AND CONSIDER

As Jesus taught in the Temple courts, the discussion shifted from the source of his teaching to the truth of his identity. Some knew Jesus was a wanted man and questioned why the Temple leadership was letting him address the crowds without arresting him. They wondered, *"Can it be true that the authorities know he is the Messiah?"* The religious leaders were afraid to arrest Jesus publicly because they didn't want to start a riot. (See John 11:47-53.) Others questioned Jesus' messianic credentials based on his origins: *"But we know where this man is from. When the Messiah comes, nobody will know where he is from."*

In the ancient world a person's family and hometown were the primary markers of identity. When you met someone, the first questions were, "Where do you come from?" and "Who is your family?" That is why Jesus was so often identified as *Jesus of Nazareth* or *Jesus, son of Joseph* or sometimes *Jesus, son of Mary.* (See John 1:45, 18:5; Luke 4:22; Mark 6:3.) But now those human markers of identity were used to deny Jesus as Messiah.

In the first century, theories about the Messiah proliferated. Most expected the Messiah to be a royal figure, descended from the family of David, who would lead a military victory over the Romans and establish a worldwide Jewish monarchy. (See 2 Samuel 7:11-17.) Others anticipated a prophetic Messiah like Moses who would lead his people from slavery to Rome into the promised land of freedom and independence. (See Deuteronomy 18:15-18.) Some believed the Messiah would be a heavenly figure in human form who would descend on clouds of glory to supernaturally establish God's rule over the nations. (See Daniel 7:13-14.)

This school of thought based on Daniel's prophecy asserted no one would know where the Messiah came from because he descended from heaven. On that basis people concluded Jesus could not be the Messiah because they knew where he grew up and who his family was. Despite his undeniable human origins, Jesus pointed to his divine origins which were unlike any on earth: *"You know me and you know where I am from. Yet I have not come on my own, but the one who sent me is true. You don't know him; I know him because I am from him, and he sent me."*

This overt claim of divinity caused such a stir that some in the crowd tried to forcibly detain Jesus. But they were not able to do so. Many in the crowd pointed to Jesus' miracles as confirmation of his messianic identity: *"When the Messiah comes, he won't perform more signs than this man has done, will he?"* All this controversy moved the religious leaders to action, and they sent the Temple police to arrest Jesus, but the police were not able to find him. Jesus said, almost taunting them, *"You will look for me, but you will not find me; and where I am, you cannot come."* This confused the crowd further, and some wondered if it meant Jesus would flee Palestine and take his ministry to the wider Gentile world. Of course, he was prophetically pointing toward his death, resurrection, and ascension, which would eventually lead to a worldwide missional movement!

The question of Jesus' identity still stirs controversy today. Was he simply a wise religious teacher or a great prophet? Was he a master of deception who fooled the masses? Was he a self-deceived savant who imagined himself to be more than he was? Many have pointed out the first theory, which is perhaps the most widespread, is not logically tenable since Jesus claimed to be more than a teacher or prophet—he claimed to be the divine Son of God descended from heaven to save the world. If we reject Jesus' own claim to be Lord, then the only reasonable conclusions are that he was a liar or a lunatic!

How do you answer the question of Jesus' identity? Is he more than just a teacher or prophet to you? If so, what does that mean for your life today?

REFLECT AND RESPOND

What is Jesus saying to me right now?

What step of faith is Jesus calling me to take today?

DAY 24

Take a minute to listen for what God is saying in these verses…

COMMENT AND CONSIDER

An ancient, stepped street leading south from the Temple Mount down through the Tyropoean Valley to the Pool of Siloam was recently discovered in Jerusalem. This pool is located at the very southern tip of the ridge known as the City of David. It was designed to collect water from the Gihon Spring. Archaeologists are currently excavating the stepped street through an underground tunnel, and soon visitors will be able to walk its entire length from the Temple to the Pool of Siloam. The road, dating from the time of Jesus, is well built, nearly perfectly preserved, and has a large drainage tunnel running underneath it.

The Festival of Shelters, also known as Tabernacles or Booths, lasted for eight days. Each day of the feast, the priests led a procession down that very stepped street from the Temple to the Pool of Siloam for a famous water-drawing ceremony. They carried large silver pitchers, scooped up water from the pool, and then returned to the inner courts of the Temple where they poured out the water at the base of the altar. Josephus, the first-century Jewish historian, tells us the High Priest had tiny golden bells sewn into the hem of his robe so he jingled as he walked. Archaeologists discovered exactly such a tiny golden bell wedged between two stones in the drainage channel underneath that street. Perhaps it was during this procession that one of those bells worked its way loose, bounced on the street, into the drain, and got stuck in a crack to be discovered some 2,000 years later!

This water-drawing ceremony was famous, not only among those who lived in Jerusalem, but also among the Jews in the wider Gentile world who heard about it from pilgrims returning from the festival. An ancient pilgrim's water flask which has been preserved displays images from the water-drawing ceremony stamped onto it. The outpouring of water at the base of the altar was evocative of the vision from Ezekiel 47, which was read during the ceremonies in the

Temple. Ezekiel saw a river flowing east from the base of the Temple, through the Kidron Valley and pouring down into the Jordan Rift Valley. This prophetic flow of water brought life and fruit to the desert, turning the Dead Sea into a freshwater lake teeming with fish. As Ezekiel prophesied, *"Since the water will become fresh, there will be life everywhere the river goes."* (Ezekiel 47:9)

It is not hard to picture the imagery Jesus was drawing on when he stood up in the Temple courts on the eighth and final day of the festival declaring, *"If anyone is thirsty, let him come to me and drink. The one who believes in me, as the Scripture has said, will have streams of living water flow from deep within him."* It is a vivid picture of living water flowing from Jesus into his followers and from them into a world desperately in need of new life! John tells us this is a picture of the Holy Spirit who now fills the heart, mind, and soul of every person who puts their trust in Jesus.

This profound image was so powerful it moved more people to recognize Jesus as the great Prophet like Moses. Others identified him as the royal Messiah descended from David, while still others claimed he couldn't be the Messiah, assuming Jesus was born in Nazareth and not in Bethlehem as the Prophet Micah foretold. There was another attempt to take Jesus into custody, but even the Temple police sent by the religious authorities were so moved by Jesus' teaching that they refused to lay a hand on him. While the chief priests and Pharisees denounced Jesus, Nicodemus took his first step toward publicly confessing his faith in Jesus by saying, *"Our law doesn't judge a man before it hears from him and knows what he's doing, does it?"* However, he was quickly shouted down by those determined to destroy Jesus.

What role does the Holy Spirit play in your life? Are you allowing the Spirit to flow from Jesus into your life and from you into the lives of others? How can you give the Spirit greater control in your life?

REFLECT AND RESPOND

What is Jesus saying to me right now?

What step of faith is Jesus calling me to take today?

FOOTSTEPS EVERY WEEK: REVIEW

Write a brief summary of what Jesus said to you each day this past week and the step of faith he called you to take:

MONDAY

TUESDAY

WEDNESDAY

THURSDAY

FRIDAY

SATURDAY

FOOTSTEPS EVERY WEEK: REFLECT

BIG PICTURE

As you look over what Jesus has said to you this past week, do you see any themes? What is the most important thing you need to remember and believe?

PREDICTABLE PATTERN

As you look over what Jesus called you to do this past week, is there a new predictable pattern he is inviting you to establish in your life with God and others?

PLANT THE WORD

As you look over the readings from this past week, write out the passage that feels most important for you and memorize it over the next week:

DAY 25

READ AND LISTEN: JOHN 7:53-8:11

Take a minute to listen for what God is saying in these verses…

COMMENT AND CONSIDER

The ancient texts of the Bible were hand-copied by skilled scribes who generally took it as a sacred calling to accurately record the words of Scripture. Occasionally variants appear in ancient texts due to scribal error or an intentional edit thought to correct an earlier error. Usually these are very minor changes that don't affect the meaning of the text. Very occasionally we find a section in the Gospels that seems to be written by a different author and attached to the current book.

Both by its omission from the earliest versions and because of a noticeably different style, most scholars conclude John 7:53-8:11 was written by someone other than John and added after the fact. However, it is included in relatively early copies and bears the marks of a genuine Gospel account, so most accept it as a credible account of an event from the life of Jesus. Perhaps this encounter took place during the same Festival of Shelters John has been recording, and a later scribe thought this was an appropriate place to insert this powerful story.

Jesus took the posture of a teacher by sitting down and began to address the people in the Temple courts when the scribes and Pharisees brought a woman before him. *"Teacher," they said to him, "this woman was caught in the act of committing adultery. In the law Moses commanded us to stone such women. So what do you say?"* Their language makes it clear the man was also caught, but the hypocrisy of her accusers is demonstrated by their failure to accuse him who was equally liable to punishment.

Exodus 20:10 prescribes death by stoning for both the male and female convicted of adultery. The Romans reserved capital punishment for their own courts. By the time of Jesus, death for adultery was rarely enforced by the Jews. (Cf. Mary's pregnancy before consummating her marriage with Joseph, Matthew 1:18-19.) However, since the Mosaic Law did call for stoning, they were testing Jesus to see if he would challenge Roman jurisdiction or compromise the demands of the Law. (See Matthew 22:15-33.) Either way they could have grounds to accuse him.

Jesus bent over in his seat and began writing in the dust on the stone paving of the Temple Courts. No one knows what he was writing, but some have speculated it was the names of those who were accusing her or a Scripture such as *"All who turn away from me will be written in the dirt, for they have abandoned the Lord, the fountain of living water."* (Jeremiah 17:13) Others have speculated he was writing the applicable commandment against adultery which God wrote with his finger on the stone tablet. (See Deuteronomy 9:10.) Perhaps the most compelling explanation is drawn from Arabic texts which demonstrate that, when a Middle Easterner is overcome by feelings they can't control, they will doodle in the dirt to regain their composure. Was Jesus so enraged by the judgmental hypocrisy of these religious men who were using a broken woman as their political pawn that he needed a few moments to regain his composure?

In any case, Jesus responded to their questions with the most profound answer imaginable, *"The one without sin among you should be the first to throw a stone at her."* The Mosaic Law declared that false witnesses should receive the same condemnation they sought to impose and that true witnesses should be the first to drop stones on the one being condemned. (See Deuteronomy 17:4-5, 19:18-19.) Jesus demonstrated they were all false witnesses liable to the very judgment they were presuming to pass on this woman. After they all walked away, silenced by the revelation of their own hypocrisy, Jesus declared his refusal to condemn her, although he is the only one worthy to do so. Instead, he gave her the redemptive admonition to receive this grace as empowerment to change: *"Go, and from now on do not sin anymore."*

Are you applying a different standard to others than you apply to yourself? What keeps you from recognizing your own sin? How can God's grace empower you to live a more Jesus-shaped life?

REFLECT AND RESPOND

What is Jesus saying to me right now?

What step of faith is Jesus calling me to take today?

DAY 26

READ AND LISTEN: JOHN 8:12-20

Take a minute to listen for what God is saying in these verses…

COMMENT AND CONSIDER

Since the first verses of John 8 were added later, we know this passage took place in the Temple Courts on the eighth and final day of the Festival of Shelters, and follows Jesus' declaration *"If anyone is thirsty, let him come to me and drink. The one who believes in me, as the Scripture has said, will have streams of living water flow from deep within him."* As we saw, this imagery was based on the famous water-drawing ceremony in which silver pitchers were filled with water from the Pool of Siloam and poured out at the base of the altar in the Court of the Priests.

Another important element of this water-pouring ritual was the lighting of the four huge lamps mounted on thirty-foot tall towers which stood in the eastern court of the Temple, known as the Court of the Women or the Treasury. They held four golden basins which served as enormous oil lamps. The Mishnah says, "the light from the candelabra was so bright that there was not a courtyard in Jerusalem that was not illuminated from the light of the Place of the Drawing of the Water." These towering lamps that lit up the city symbolized the pillar of fire that led the people through the Sinai wilderness.

But the lamps were not the only use of fire during the celebration of Shelters. According to the Mishnah, in addition to the pouring out of the water pitchers, the priests "would dance before the people who attended the celebration, with flaming torches that they would juggle in their hands, and they would say before them passages of song and praise to God. And the Levites would play on lyres, harps, cymbals, and trumpets, and countless other musical instruments." John adds the note, *He spoke these words by the treasury, while teaching in the temple,* to make it clear that Jesus' teaching was happening in the same place these symbolic rituals had been taking place every day during the festival.

So, when Jesus said, *"I am the light of the world. Anyone who follows me will never walk in the darkness but will have the light of life"* the connection was crystal clear. Jesus is the pillar of fire who turns our darkness to light! His light makes us fully alive! Jesus will light our way when we are lost in the wilderness. Jesus will scatter the darkness and lead us into the light of God's truth. These are Jesus' promises to us as we trust him enough to follow him by faith.

Of course, this powerful message evoked a defensive reaction from the Pharisees. They said, *"You are testifying about yourself. Your testimony is not valid."* When they challenged Jesus' testimony earlier, he lifted up four witnesses which testify to his true identity: John the Baptist, his own works, his heavenly Father, and the Word of God. (See John 5:31-40.) When they complained that they knew where he came from, he told them his true origin was from the Father. (See John 7:28-29.) Now Jesus reiterated, *"My testimony is true, because I know where I came from and where I'm going."*

The Law required two witnesses who agree to prove your case in court. (See Deuteronomy 19:15.) So, he gave them two witnesses, himself and his father. But then, perhaps as a slur on Jesus' legitimacy given the circumstances of Mary's pregnancy, they said, *"Where is your Father?"* Jesus replied, *"You know neither me nor my Father… If you knew me, you would also know my Father."* He didn't need anyone else's affirmation, because his heavenly Father had already revealed his identity and calling. The secret of Jesus' authority and power was that he knew who he was and knew his purpose.

Are you secure enough in your identity and calling to overcome those who question who you are and what you are about? In what way is Jesus scattering your darkness and showing you the way? What does it mean for you to walk in the light of life?

REFLECT AND RESPOND

What is Jesus saying to me right now?

What step of faith is Jesus calling me to take today?

DAY 27

READ AND LISTEN: JOHN 8:21-29

Take a minute to listen for what God is saying in these verses…

COMMENT AND CONSIDER

Jesus lived with a vivid sense of his destiny and calling. Even as a boy, he knew who he was and what he was to be about. (See Luke 2:46.) As the religious and political opposition grew, so did Jesus' awareness that his end was drawing near. Perhaps his cousin John's prophecy at the Jordan River was still ringing in his ears, *"Look, the Lamb of God, who takes away the sin of the world!"* (John 1:29) Jesus knew he was soon going to die as the perfect sacrifice for all of humanity.

As Jesus' earthly end became more vivid to him, so did his earthly beginning. Jesus was profoundly aware he had existed before his birth in Bethlehem. He knew his biological family back in Nazareth was not his primary family. He knew he had come from the Father and was going back to the Father. Jesus' death would not end as our deaths do here on earth. Jesus knew he was going to rise from the dead as the first fruits of the New Creation, fully alive, never to die again! Then he would ascend to the right hand of the Father and take his rightful role as King of the Universe.

As Jesus engaged with the crowds who filled the Temple Courts, the religious leaders became increasingly antagonistic. Perhaps it was with a sense of sadness Jesus said to them, *"I'm going away; you will look for me, and you will die in your sin. Where I'm going, you cannot come."* But they continued to taunt him, framing his statements as suicidal. Jesus replied by pointing to his preexistence, *"You are from below… I am from above. You are of this world; I am not of this world."* Despite their hostile scorn, he offered them a lifeline, *"For if you do not believe that I am he, you will die in your sins."*

The phrase *"I am he"* was a loaded one. The Greek words are *ego eimi*, "I am," which was used to translate the personal name of God, Yahweh. Jesus was hinting at his true identity as the fully divine incarnate Son of God. He was on very thin ice here. If he openly testified to his full divinity, the religious leaders would have their excuse to arrest Jesus and have him executed. But Jesus knew his mission was not yet complete, or as John put it, *his hour had not yet come.* (John 8:20) Jesus had to be very careful how he answered their question, *"Who are you?"* Instead of pointing to himself, he pointed to his Father in heaven. *"…the one who sent me is true, and what I have heard from him— these things I tell the world."*

Jesus was always clear that on this earth he operated in complete submission to and dependence on his Father. This is because he came to show us how we are to live. In his full humanity, Jesus lived the way we are meant to live. He simply listened for what his Father was saying and watched for what his Father was doing, and he did and said those things. After referring again to his divinity (*"I am he"*), he reiterated the example he was setting for us to follow: *"I do nothing on my own. But just as the Father taught me, I say these things… I always do what pleases him."*

As Jesus said so clearly, only by putting our faith in him will we escape dying in our sins. He also clearly shows us how we are to live that life of faith in him. Listening for what the Father is saying and responding to that in faith is how Jesus —and it is how we are called to live.

Do you believe Jesus is who he said he was, the divine Son of God? Are you listening for his voice today? Are you willing to exercise your faith by following his voice one step at a time?

REFLECT AND RESPOND

What is Jesus saying to me right now?

What step of faith is Jesus calling me to take today?

DAY 28

READ AND LISTEN: JOHN 8:30-38

Take a minute to listen for what God is saying in these verses…

COMMENT AND CONSIDER

John tells us that many in the holiday crowd filling the Temple Courts accepted what Jesus said and believed it was true. However, Jesus was looking for more than simple agreement with his words. He was looking for disciples who would submit to him and follow him even if they didn't fully understand everything he was saying. He was calling them into a relationship of trust. *"If you continue in my word, you really are my disciples. You will know the truth, and the truth will set you free."*

In Jewish thought "truth" is not just an objective idea that exists in a vacuum like Greek philosophy. Truth in Judaism is the rightness of a relationship founded on things being the way they were meant to be. When we begin to live according to the truth with one another, then we are beginning to know the truth. Jesus called the people in the crowd who resonated with his teaching into an ongoing relationship of faith. To *continue* in Jesus' word is to walk with him so closely that we keep hearing his voice and keep learning to follow his way. Jesus said this kind of discipleship, continuing in his word, is the only way to come to know the deeper truth and live in true freedom.

Jesus' reference to freedom pushed a button, causing some in the crowd to protest, *"We are descendants of Abraham… and we have never been enslaved to anyone."* Historically this was complete denial, since Israel had been enslaved over the centuries by Egypt, Assyria, Babylon, Persia, and Greece. Roman soldiers were looking down on the crowd at that moment from their perch in the Antonia fortress, watchful for any signs of rebellion to Caesar's current rule. Perhaps those who protested were pointing out they had never personally been legally enslaved, even though they were living under the oppression of a foreign power. But either way, they missed the point as usual. Jesus clarified, *"Truly I tell you, everyone who commits sin is a slave of sin."*

Living in sin robs us of our true humanity by separating us from the God who created us, who sustains us, and who alone can fulfill us with a truly fruitful life. Those who live in sin are subjected to the worst kind of slavery that only degrades us and further subjects us to its bondage. Most extended families included enslaved people who could be sold or released at any time. Even if slaves were included in the extended family household for a time, there was no guarantee they would continue to be part of that family in the future. A legal son, on the other hand, will be part of that family forever, both he and his descendants. Because Jesus invites us into the family of God as true sons and daughters, he offers a freedom that continues forever! He concluded, *"So if the Son sets you free, you really will be free."*

Jesus acknowledged their ethnic heritage when he conceded, *"I know you are descendants of Abraham."* But his point was that biological descent does not determine your place in God's great family. It is not enough to trace your lineage back to Abraham. The truth is we are all born into sin, and so we are all born into slavery, no matter our physical heritage. There is a new birth from above that determines your spiritual heritage. Only through the Son of God can you be reborn as sons and daughters of your heavenly Father. Only by taking up your place in his eternal family will you be set free forever!

Do you simply agree with Jesus' words, or are you continuing to listen and trust his word as you follow him, even if you don't always understand? Have you been born again into your new identity as a son or daughter of God? Are you living in the freedom that can only be found by taking up your rightful place in God's great family?

REFLECT AND RESPOND

What is Jesus saying to me right now?

What step of faith is Jesus calling me to take today?

DAY 29

READ AND LISTEN: JOHN 8:39-47

Take a minute to listen for what God is saying in these verses…

COMMENT AND CONSIDER

It was still early in Jesus' ministry when the religious leaders began plotting with the ruling Herodian party about how they were going to have Jesus killed. (See Mark 3:6; John 5:18.) By ignoring the Pharisees' flawed interpretation of the Law and healing people on the Sabbath, Jesus had mounted a direct challenge to their authority. As a result, the Pharisees decided to get rid of him in order to maintain their own position and power. Jesus was well aware of these dangerous political currents and had delayed his arrival in Jerusalem for the Festival of Shelters in order to dodge the authorities. Even now he chose his words with excruciating care to avoid giving the leaders an excuse to arrest him.

Jesus consistently referred to God as his own Father and the Source of his teaching, but they rejected this identification. They taunted him saying, *"Where is your Father?"* (John 8:19) This was an attempt to call Jesus' patrimony as well as his teaching into question. Joseph had apparently died sometime after Jesus was 12, and there were persistent rumors he wasn't Jesus' natural father anyway. By contrast the religious authorities said, "Our father is Abraham." But Jesus challenged this identification, not on natural grounds, but because they did not do what Abraham did. Instead, Jesus hinted that they were imitating a different, more sinister father. (See verse 44.)

Abraham was lifted up by first-century Jews as a paragon of virtue, especially of righteousness and faithfulness. Moses tells us the source of these virtues was Abraham's covenantal relationship with God established through faith: *Abram believed the Lord, and he credited it to him as righteousness.* (Genesis 15:6) These religious leaders did not come to Jesus with an attitude of faith, but rather with fear, pride, and duplicity. They may have been Abraham's biological children, but now they imitated a very different father, the father of lies.

The religious leaders responded to Jesus' challenge by going back on the offensive with their smear campaign. *"We weren't born of sexual immorality," they said.* Their implication was that Jesus' mother had committed adultery in conceiving him, just about the worst insult a first-century Jew could hurl at another. Later rabbis claimed Mary conceived Jesus with a Roman soldier, a desperate attempt to invalidate his identity and authority. Then they tried to turn the tables on Jesus by adopting his claim as their own, *"We have one Father—God."* Jesus pointed out if this were true, they would be enjoying a very different kind of conversation! *"If God were your Father, you would love me, because I came from God and I am here."*

Earlier, when the Pharisees had accused Jesus of being possessed by demons, he warned them, *"whoever blasphemes against the Holy Spirit never has forgiveness, but is guilty of an eternal sin"—because they were saying, "He has an unclean spirit."* (Mark 3:29-30) But now, because they claimed to follow God as their Father while rejecting Jesus' identity as Son of the Father, Jesus took the bold step of naming the true inspiration of their constant opposition to his mission: *"You are of your father the devil, and you want to carry out your father's desires. He was a murderer from the beginning and does not stand in the truth, because there is no truth in him. When he tells a lie, he speaks from his own nature, because he is a liar and the father of lies."* Far from blasphemy of the Spirit, this unflinching diagnosis was the correct discernment of spirits.

Jesus was able to discern which voice was his Father's and which was from the father of lies. This is how he was able to overcome the direct attack on his identity by which the enemy was trying to undermine and destroy him through lies.

Are you learning to recognize the voice of your Father speaking truth to you through his Word and Spirit? How can you build your identity on that truth by rejecting the lies of the enemy aimed at undermining your identity and authority as a child of God?

REFLECT AND RESPOND

What is Jesus saying to me right now?

What step of faith is Jesus calling me to take today?

DAY 30

READ AND LISTEN: JOHN 8:48-59

Take a minute to listen for what God is saying in these verses…

COMMENT AND CONSIDER

Ancient rhetoricians taught their students to return the accusations of their opponents back on them. Jesus had just called the religious leaders children of the devil, and now they lamely tried to turn the charge back on Jesus, throwing in an ethnic insult for good measure: *"Aren't we right in saying that you're a Samaritan and have a demon?"* Jesus let the truth of his message and the integrity of his actions be the self-evident proof of his character. Jesus didn't point to himself; he always pointed to his Father in heaven on whom he relied for everything. Jesus honored and glorified the Father, but these religious leaders dishonored his Son in the worst possible ways, calling him illegitimate, identifying him with the hated Samaritans, and accusing him of demonization.

Rather than intimidating Jesus, these accusations emboldened him to be even more forthcoming about his identity and mission. *"Truly I tell you, if anyone keeps my word, he will never see death."* This is a bold claim indeed! Death is the great equalizer before which both kings and peasants must bow. Death is the one inevitability from which no amount of money, power, or fame can save us. But Jesus claimed that keeping his word was enough to overcome the greatest power on earth. Years later, the writer of Hebrews put it this way: *"Now since the children have flesh and blood in common, Jesus also shared in these, so that through his death he might destroy the one holding the power of death—that is, the devil—and free those who were held in slavery all their lives by the fear of death."* (Hebrews 2:14-15)

Jesus said the key that destroys the effects of death and unlocks this indestructible kind of life that not even the devil can steal is *"if anyone keeps my word."* Keeping Jesus' word means not only to receive that word, but to respond to it, allowing the word to shape our character and empower our actions. Jesus told the religious leaders this was precisely their problem: *"my word has no place among you"* (John 8:37) But those who trust Jesus by receiving and responding to his word are made one with him in the New Covenant. Jesus' life becomes our life! Jesus' resurrection becomes our resurrection! In this way, those who keep Jesus' word will never succumb to the power of death.

This was the religious leaders' last chance to repent of their diabolical opposition to Jesus by receiving and responding to his word. Instead, they doubled down on their accusations against him. *"Now we know you have a demon."* Since even Abraham himself died, they rightly perceived Jesus was claiming to be greater than their greatest patriarch. Unable to comprehend what Jesus was saying, they asked, *"Who do you claim to be?"* He told them Abraham had prophetically seen the day of Jesus' coming, just as he foresaw the 400-year Egyptian slavery of Israel and their exodus back to the promised land of Canaan. (See Genesis 15:12-21.) Incredulous, they replied, *"You aren't fifty years old yet, and you've seen Abraham?"* Unable to deny himself, Jesus unmistakably stated his pre-existent divinity by answering, *"Truly I tell you, before Abraham was, I am."*

If he just wanted to claim pre-existence, Jesus would have said "before Abraham was, I was." By saying *"before Abraham was, I am"* he clearly defined himself as the fully divine, pre-existent, incarnate Son of God. The religious leaders understood this and picked up stones to kill him. Blind to the glory being revealed to them by the Father, these religious leaders tragically committed blasphemy against the Holy Spirit by rejecting the One who was infinitely greater than Abraham and all the prophets. (See Mark 3:29-30.) We would be wise to heed this warning and learn from their mistake by letting Jesus continually reveal himself to us, so we might keep growing in our understanding and appreciation of who he really is!

Do you have presuppositions about Jesus that don't match his self-revelation? How can you let him teach you to know him more fully? What does it mean for you to keep his word today?

REFLECT AND RESPOND

What is Jesus saying to me right now?

What step of faith is Jesus calling me to take today?

FOOTSTEPS EVERY WEEK: REVIEW

Write a brief summary of what Jesus said to you each day this past week and the step of faith he called you to take:

MONDAY

TUESDAY

WEDNESDAY

THURSDAY

FRIDAY

SATURDAY

Footsteps Every Week: Reflect

Big Picture
As you look over what Jesus has said to you this past week, do you see any themes? What is the most important thing you need to remember and believe?

Predictable Pattern
As you look over what Jesus called you to do this past week, is there a new predictable pattern he is inviting you to establish in your life with God and others?

Plant the Word
As you look over the readings from this past week, write out the passage that feels most important for you and memorize it over the next week:

DAY 31

READ AND LISTEN: JOHN 9:1-12

Take a minute to listen for what God is saying in these verses…

COMMENT AND CONSIDER

Jesus managed to slip out of the Temple Courts, hidden from the sight of the angry religious leaders who wanted to stone him for blasphemy. Perhaps it was on their way down the huge staircase leading south from the Temple's Double Gate that Jesus and the disciples passed a man born blind who was strategically positioned to beg from worshipers heading up to worship God at the Temple. Assuming his condition was a direct punishment for sin, the disciples wondered specifically whose sin was responsible for this man's condition. They asked Jesus, *"Rabbi, who sinned, this man or his parents, that he was born blind?"* Jesus responded by refuting their assumption that human suffering is divine punishment, *"Neither this man nor his parents sinned."* Instead, Jesus saw this man's condition as an opportunity to demonstrate the power of God and the nature of his Kingdom.

In the ancient world, artificial light was weak and difficult to maintain. Therefore, most activities ceased when the sun went down unless there was an emergency. Jesus explained the urgency of the Kingdom when he said, *"We must do the works of him who sent me while it is day. Night is coming when no one can work."* There is a limited window of time for us to demonstrate the Kingdom of God to a broken and dying world, and we are called to make the most of the time we have been given.

Each day of the Festival of Shelters, a spectacular torchlight dancing ceremony took place in the Temple's Court of Women, commemorating the pillar of fire that led the people of Israel through the wilderness. This inner court is where Jesus had been teaching on that eighth and final day of the festival, so it is not surprising he drew upon the imagery of light to address the blind man's condition. Speaking against the darkness which had engulfed this man since birth, Jesus declared, *"I am the light of the world."*

Spitting on the ground, Jesus made mud and applied it to the blind man's eyes, then told him "Go, wash in the pool of Siloam." Archaeologists recently uncovered remains of the Pool of Siloam from the time of Jesus in the southernmost tip of the City of David, the oldest part of Jerusalem. There Herod built a large, stepped pool which captured the water flowing from the Gihon Spring through the ancient tunnel cut by King Hezekiah to bring spring water inside the city walls. Even more recently archaeologists discovered a beautifully preserved first-century stepped street that leads from the Temple Mount southward down the ridge of the City of David to the Pool of Siloam. This is the very street the blind man used to make his way from the Temple to the pool.

It is noteworthy that this blind man was willing to navigate the hundreds of steps, countless shops, and crowds of people carrying water jars up and down that street. He trusted Jesus enough to act on his word. Reaching the Pool of Siloam, he felt his way down the steps to the water's edge, bent down, washed away the spit-made mud, opened his eyes, blinked in the sunlight, and saw that Jesus really is the Light of the World! I love walking up that ancient stepped-street, imagining this used-to-be blind man running and jumping two steps at a time, shouting for joy and hugging strangers on his way back up to the Temple and a whole new life!

By faith the power of Jesus flowed through this man's heart and literally recreated his eyes. When people began asking him what had happened, he immediately testified to the work of Jesus in his life. What a contrast to the paralyzed man in John 5 who not only demonstrated no faith in Jesus at all, even after his miraculous healing, but then reported Jesus to the religious authorities! (See John 5:1-16.)

Are you willing to act on Jesus' word to you, even if it feels difficult or seems ridiculous? Do you openly testify to the good work Jesus has done in your life, or do you let those opportunities slip away?

REFLECT AND RESPOND

What is Jesus saying to me right now?

What step of faith is Jesus calling me to take today?

DAY 32

READ AND LISTEN: JOHN 9:13-34

Take a minute to listen for what God is saying in these verses…

COMMENT AND CONSIDER

Jesus' primary operating principle was simply to perceive what his heavenly Father was doing and then to join him in that Kingdom activity. (See John 5:19.) This principle superseded the many religious rules which the rabbis added to the written Law of the Old Testament. Often this meant Jesus did things on the Sabbath which did not violate the spirit of the written Sabbath Law but broke the religious rules of the scribes and Pharisees. Jesus explained why he healed people on the Sabbath when he said, *"My Father is still working, and I am working also."* (John 5:17) The day Jesus healed the man born blind happened to be a Sabbath day. When people told the Pharisees what Jesus had done, they immediately began to investigate Jesus for breaking their rules.

When the religious authorities began to interrogate him about his healing, the man simply reported what he had experienced. *"He put mud on my eyes,"* he told them. *"I washed and I can see."* This is an important principle in sharing our faith. You don't need to be a Bible expert or a persuasive speaker to communicate the Good News of Jesus to those who don't know him. All you need to do is tell people what Jesus has done in your life and how you have changed. In a court of law, witnesses are those who testify to what they have seen and heard. This is what it means to be a faithful witness.

But even the stupendous miracle of a man blind from birth receiving his sight was not enough to move the stubborn hearts of these rabbis. They began debating whether someone who failed to keep their religious rules could possibly exercise the supernatural power to do God's will. When they pressed the formerly blind man for his evaluation of Jesus, he simply said, *"He's a prophet."* So they decided to expand their investigation and called in the man's parents. His mother and father passed the buck back to their son because they were afraid of being excluded from the synagogue. This was a real threat, because later in the first century Jewish followers of Jesus in the synagogue were tested by being made to read a list of blessings and curses, the final of which declared a curse against those who followed Jesus. If they refused to read this final curse out loud, they were expelled from the synagogue.

The Pharisees decided to cross-examine the healed man once again, pressuring him to denounce Jesus, *"Give glory to God. We know that this man is a sinner."* The used-to-be blind man responded, *"Whether or not he's a sinner, I don't know. One thing I do know: I was blind, and now I can see!"* Although he didn't feel qualified to make a complex theological argument about Jesus' identity, he continued to give the simple, undeniable testimony about what Jesus had done in his life. They tried to intimidate him to give in, but the formerly blind man challenged them to respond to Jesus, *"Why do you want to hear it again? You don't want to become his disciples too, do you?"* The Pharisees responded by defensively identifying themselves as disciples of Moses rather than Jesus.

Despite their ridicule and intimidation, this man patiently went on to explain the logic of Jesus' credibility. Since Jesus undeniably performed this first-ever-in-history miracle, it is clear he is a genuine and trustworthy representative of God who speaks the truth. The clarity of this logic was too compelling for these teachers to refute, so they responded by expelling him from the synagogue.

Sometimes when we give our testimony, others will challenge the validity of our message, and we need to be prepared to answer the charges which may be brought against us. We are called to be as steadfast and persistent in sharing the Good News as this man, but in the end how people respond to Jesus is not our responsibility. Are you willing to persist in sharing the Good News even when others try to intimidate you into silence? How can you be prepared to respond to objections others might raise as skeptics of your witness?

Reflect and Respond

What is Jesus saying to me right now?

What step of faith is Jesus calling me to take today?

DAY 33

READ AND LISTEN: JOHN 9:35-41

Take a minute to listen for what God is saying in these verses…

COMMENT AND CONSIDER

Still today, three times a day observant Jews recite a series of 18 ancient prayers, in the morning, afternoon, and evening. These are referred to as the "Eighteen Benedictions" or the *Adimah*. In the first century, these prayers were recited out loud at the end of the synagogue service. Sometime before the destruction of the Temple in AD 70, an extra prayer was added as a curse against heretics; it has become the 14th Benediction. It reads, "For the apostates let there be no hope, and may the kingdom of the arrogant be quickly uprooted in our days; and may the *Nazarim* and *Minim* instantly perish; may they be blotted from the book of the living, and not be written with the righteous."

Minim means "heretics," and *Nazarim* refers to the early followers of Jesus, the Nazarene. The insertion of these curses was a reaction to the growing movement of Jesus' followers within Judaism in the first century and was used to identify those in the synagogue who believed Jesus was the Messiah. If someone was suspected of being a disciple of Jesus, they were asked to recite the Eighteen Benedictions at the end of the service. If they refused, they were excommunicated from the synagogue on the assumption they were one of the *Minim/Nazarim*. This inserted curse of the "heretics" was not universally applied until after the destruction of the Temple, but even before AD 70 it was used selectively in synagogues which were determined to root out early Jewish Christians.

John tells us *"the Jews had already agreed that if anyone confessed him as the Messiah, he would be banned from the synagogue."* (John 9:22) This is a clue that a more systematic expulsion of Jesus' followers was taking place in western Asia Minor around the great city of Ephesus where John lived when he was writing his Gospel. For these Jews who had been expelled from the synagogue because of their faith in Jesus, the fact that this formerly blind man was expelled as well would have given them a profound connection to the story. That Jesus went and found this man and welcomed him into his spiritual family would have been a great encouragement and comfort to these persecuted Jewish followers of Jesus. When we are rejected for our testimony of Jesus, it is so good to know that he will never forsake us but offers us a place in God's great family where we belong forever! (See John 14:1-6.)

When Jesus found the used-to-be blind man, he shared a more complete Gospel with him. All the man knew was that Jesus was a Prophet who had given him his sight. But now Jesus took him deeper in discipleship, inviting him to put his faith in the Son of Man. The man's response demonstrated an open heart and willing spirit, *"Who is he, Sir, that I may believe in him?"* When Jesus pointed to himself, the eyes of this man's heart were fully opened, and he not only declared his faith in Jesus but also began to worship him! Here we see his journey from respecting Jesus as a Prophet sent by God to recognizing him as the fully divine Messianic King deserving of our complete trust and worship.

Jesus declared that this man's spiritual blindness was now gone, and some of the Pharisees who were listening to all this were so moved they asked, *"We aren't blind too, are we?"* Jesus responded, *"If you were blind," Jesus told them, "you wouldn't have sin. But now that you say, 'We see,' your sin remains."* Religious pride keeps the spiritually blind from seeing, but genuine humility opens the eyes of our hearts to see Jesus for who he really is. When our posture toward Jesus is "Who are you Lord, that I might know you," he is faithful to lead us deeper into the wonder of his true identity and the power of his Kingdom.

Are you open to a new and deeper revelation of who Jesus really is? Are you welcoming others who might be cast out and rejected to join you as a part of God's eternal family?

REFLECT AND RESPOND

What is Jesus saying to me right now?

What step of faith is Jesus calling me to take today?

DAY 34

READ AND LISTEN: JOHN 10:1-9

Take a minute to listen for what God is saying in these verses…

COMMENT AND CONSIDER

The Hebrew Scriptures are rich with imagery drawn from the familiar Middle Eastern image of a shepherd caring for his sheep. God is pictured as the Shepherd of his people, and Israel is depicted as his flock. (See Genesis 48:15 and Psalm 78:52 for examples.) When the leaders of Israel abused God's people and led them astray, they were described as wicked shepherds. (See Ezekiel 34:2-10.) David, the shepherd boy who became a king, gave the most famous depiction of God as the ultimate Shepherd in his famous 23rd Psalm: *"The Lord is my shepherd; I have what I need. He lets me lie down in green pastures; he leads me beside quiet waters. He renews my life…"* (Psalms 23:1-3) Given this rich imagery, it is not surprising that Jesus drew upon these pastoral images from everyday life to describe his relationship with those who follow him.

The job of the biblical shepherd was to protect and provide for the sheep. The way the shepherd protected his sheep at night was by building a sheep pen to keep them safe from thieves and predators. This was normally a stone-walled compound connected to the extended family home. Sometimes thornbushes were placed at the top of the wall for further protection. A strong wooden door that could be locked with iron bars prevented animals or thieves from breaking in to attack the flock. Just such an animal pen was attached to the eastern wall of the house of Simon and Andrew in Capernaum. And it was in an area like this in the extended family home of Joseph in Bethlehem where Mary gave birth to Jesus and laid him in a stone manger, *"because there was no guest room available for them."* (Luke 2:7)

While the sheep pen provided protection, it afforded no food for the flock. So the shepherd opened the door each morning and led the flock from the pen into pastures where they could find grass and water, bringing them back to the pen before dark. Sometimes the shepherd led the flock from the back, poking and prodding them with his staff, to get them out of their comfortable pen and into the fields. Then he shifted to the front of the flock to show them the right path which led to green pastures and still waters. All the while the shepherd called his sheep by name, because he knew his sheep, and they recognized his voice. In nearly 40 years of traveling in biblical lands, I have seen this scene played out countless times, virtually unchanged since time immemorial.

During the winter months, enough grass grew on the hills surrounding the village that the shepherd could lead his flock out from the extended family home each morning, then bring them back at night. But as spring turned into summer, grass was harder to find, and the shepherd would have to take his flock farther away, too far to return home each night. During these dry months, the shepherd constructed a simple sheep pen in front of a cave or in the open field, stacking stones and thornbushes into a circle with a single opening where the shepherd would sleep.

Like a shepherd calling his sheep out of their pen, Jesus called out to the fishermen on the shore of the Sea of Galilee, *"Follow me."* He stood outside Matthew's tax collection booth and called out, *"Follow me."* These were the first sheep to recognize Jesus' voice as the voice of their Shepherd and to respond by following him. Many more joined them, and he calls to us still today. The question is will we recognize his voice and follow? Like the shepherd sleeping across the opening of the pen, there is only one way into Jesus' flock—through him. He is *"the gate for the sheep."* As he told them in the upper room, *"No one comes to the Father except through me."* (John 14:6)

Have you entered God's flock through faith in Jesus your Good Shepherd? Are you looking to him for your protection and provision? How are you recognizing Jesus' voice and following in his Way?

REFLECT AND RESPOND

What is Jesus saying to me right now?

What step of faith is Jesus calling me to take today?

DAY 35

Take a minute to listen for what God is saying in these verses…

COMMENT AND CONSIDER

When first-century Jews thought of "the good shepherd," they immediately pictured the ideal Shepherd David depicted in his most-famous Psalm 23. The good shepherd leads his flock through the darkest valleys to find abundant water and grass. As spring moves toward summer, in the Middle East grass becomes scarce. Ground water collects down in the bottom of the wadis, the desert valleys cut by seasonal runoff. This is where the experienced shepherd could find food and water even in the dry summer and fall months.

However, the wadis were dangerous because this is also where predators hid, ready to pounce on the flock which could not escape due to the steep walls of the valley. When unexpected thunderstorms hit, the wadis are also where powerful flash floods can form and wash away any creature in its path. Still today, people are killed in the Judean desert nearly every year from these flash floods.

Yet when the good shepherd is leading them, the sheep do not fear the dangers of the valley of the shadow of death, because they know their shepherd will protect them. The two primary tools of the shepherd are his rod and staff. The rod is a club with a leather wrist strap that can be swung or spun and launched like a missile to take down even the most ferocious predator. The staff is a long walking stick used to poke and prod the sheep to keep them on the right path. By inviting the sheep into his circle of protection (the rod) and challenging the sheep to follow him on the right path (the staff), the good shepherd protects and provides for the sheep even in the most dangerous wadis.

Jesus contrasted this familiar image of the good shepherd with two other images: the thief and the hired hand. The thief does not use the gate of the sheep pen, because he has no legal right to the sheep. Instead, he slips over the wall at night to steal the sheep. (See John 10:1, 8.) Rather than providing for the sheep, the thief's purpose is to *"steal and kill and destroy"* the flock. The hired hand is only interested in his pay and is not willing to risk his life for the sheep. At the first sign of danger, the hired hand will desert the sheep to save himself. The good shepherd loves his sheep. He knows each one by name, provides for them, and is ready to risk his very life to protect them from the wolves.

Jesus wanted the crowds in the Temple Courts to be clear about his motives and his commitment to those who follow him: *"I am the good shepherd."* He loves his followers and is committed to protecting and providing for them. He is the one who will show us where to find green pasture and still water, even in the parched seasons of life. He is the one who will lead us through the dangers of the wadi on the right paths. When the wolf attacks, he will stand his ground and protect us with his rod. Our Good Shepherd has come so that we *"may have life and have it in abundance."*

Jesus was also clear about who his flock is. The Jews were chosen by God, not to exclude others, but that they might be a blessing and light to all the families of the earth. (See Genesis 12:3.) Jesus wanted this Jewish crowd to understand he was the Shepherd of the Gentiles too and would call them into one flock, one family. He would have to lay down his life to protect his flocks and form them into one, but he was choosing this fate; it was not forced on him. People in the crowd reacted in different ways to these words. Some received his message on the basis of his works, while others accused him of being demonized.

Do you believe Jesus will provide for you and protect you if you follow him? Can you discern the voice of the Shepherd from the thief and the hired hand? What does it mean for you to submit to the Good Shepherd today?

REFLECT AND RESPOND

What is Jesus saying to me right now?

What step of faith is Jesus calling me to take today?

DAY 36

READ AND LISTEN: JOHN 10:22-29

Take a minute to listen for what God is saying in these verses…

COMMENT AND CONSIDER

In 336 BC, at the age of 20 Alexander the Great began a military campaign in which he conquered land stretching from Greece to India. Before dying prematurely in 323 BC at the age of 33, he entrusted portions of his territory to various generals. Syria was ruled by Seleucus I Nicator, who established the Seleucid Empire. Initially Judea was ruled by Ptolemy of Egypt, but at the start of the second century BC, the Seleucids conquered Jerusalem. In 168 BC the Seleucid King Antiochus IV Epiphanes began violently repressing the practice of Judaism, setting up an idol of Zeus in the Temple and sacrificing pigs on the altar. This sparked a popular Jewish revolt against the Seleucids culminating in a dramatic victory by the Maccabees in 164 BC. When they cleansed and rededicated the Temple, there was only enough consecrated oil to light the Temple lamp for one day, but miraculously it burned for eight days and nights.

The Festival of Hannukah is a commemoration of the Maccabean victory and subsequent rededication of the Temple. In the first century, it involved the festive lighting of many lamps, and it was a popular follow up to the Festival of Shelters, although less important. John tells us Jesus visited Jerusalem again during this Festival of Dedication. Since it falls during the month of December, the weather had turned cold and rainy. The Temple Courts were surrounded by huge colonnades, the eastern of which was called Solomon's Portico because it was the oldest. This is where Jesus walked and taught, protected from the winter wind and rain. This is also where the crowds confronted him with the question on everyone's mind: *"If you are the Messiah, tell us plainly."*

Jesus continued striking the delicate balance between self-revelation and self-preservation. If he withheld the truth of his identity, he couldn't complete his mission, but if he revealed too much too soon, he would be arrested before he could complete the work he was sent to do. Jesus responded by pointing out that his actions clearly identified who he was. If they couldn't recognize him, that simply meant they were not part of his flock. *"My sheep hear my voice, I know them, and they follow me."* Discerning Jesus' voice and imitating his example are the primary factors that determine who are part of his flock and who are not. With that identity as his sheep comes the amazing promise, *"I give them eternal life, and they will never perish."*

This is the abundant life Jesus promised to those of us who follow the Good Shepherd. (See John 10:10.) He will lead us into green pastures which are so verdant that we can eat our fill and then lie down in the lush grass. He will lead us beside quiet waters where we can drink until our thirst is fully quenched. (See Psalm 23.) This is where the thief cannot *"steal and kill and destroy."* (John 10:10) The wolf will never snatch these sheep out his hand.

Jesus was making it clear who he really is. He is the anointed royal Messiah who has come to lead his people into lives of fruitfulness and meaning. He has come to set us free from the destructive work of our enemy the thief. His redemption is so complete that nothing can steal his sheep away from his beloved flock, not even the prowling wolf. Not ever. This is the sure and certain promise Jesus makes to everyone who recognizes who he is and chooses to submit and follow his voice.

Are you part of Jesus' flock? Are you listening for his voice? Do you trust him enough to follow where he leads? If so, nothing and no one will be able to steal you from his loving hands.

REFLECT AND RESPOND

What is Jesus saying to me right now?

What step of faith is Jesus calling me to take today?

Footsteps Every Week: Review

Write a brief summary of what Jesus said to you each day this past week and the step of faith he called you to take:

Monday

Tuesday

Wednesday

Thursday

Friday

Saturday

FOOTSTEPS EVERY WEEK: REFLECT

BIG PICTURE

As you look over what Jesus has said to you this past week, do you see any themes? What is the most important thing you need to remember and believe?

PREDICTABLE PATTERN

As you look over what Jesus called you to do this past week, is there a new predictable pattern he is inviting you to establish in your life with God and others?

PLANT THE WORD

As you look over the readings from this past week, write out the passage that feels most important for you and memorize it over the next week:

DAY 37

READ AND LISTEN: JOHN 10:30-42

Take a minute to listen for what God is saying in these verses…

COMMENT AND CONSIDER

Covenants were how biblical people related to each other. When two parties made promises to each other and trusted those promises, they were bound together in the oneness of a covenantal relationship. This applied to marriages, neighbors, business partners, nations, and God. Jesus established a New Covenant with God in his baptism, and that relationship defined his identity. The heavens opened, the Holy Spirit was poured out, and the Father spoke over the Son, *"This is my beloved Son, with whom I am well-pleased."* (Matthew 3:16-17)

When Jesus said, *"I and the Father are one,"* he was describing both his covenantal relationship with the Father and his identity as the Son. In his baptism he showed us by example how to enter the New Covenant where we can establish a relationship with God and discover our true identity as his beloved daughters and sons. But now he was saying more. We can become sons and daughters of God by grace in this New Covenant, but Jesus claimed to be *the Son of God.* He claimed a unique identity and relationship with the Father. This is why people picked up stones to throw at him. They considered Jesus' claim to a unique oneness with the Father and divine identity as *the* Son to be blasphemy.

Jesus pointed out the irony of stoning a man who only ever did good, showed compassion, and acted in love toward others. *"I have shown you many good works from the Father. For which of these works are you stoning me?"* Jesus' extraordinary life was the confirmation of his divine identity and unique relationship to the Father. But that wasn't enough for these people. Jesus didn't fit their theological categories. He didn't follow their religious rules. He challenged their assumptions. So they tried to kill him.

In the ancient world, it was assumed that kings sat among the council of the gods and so were considered divine. David wrote in Psalm 110:1: *This is the declaration of the Lord to my Lord: "Sit at my right hand until I make your enemies your footstool."* Jesus used that verse to point out that the Jewish people should have expected a divine Messiah because David referred to the Messiah as "my Lord," even though the Messiah is a descendant of David. (See Matthew 22:41-46.) Jesus used the inspired Scriptures to show people that their assumptions were wrong and that God was doing something they never expected.

Here Jesus quotes another Psalm to stretch the thinking of the crowds about his identity and divinity. In Psalm 82:1 it says, *God stands in the divine assembly; he pronounces judgment among the gods.* In this context the "gods" are either a royal court of heavenly angels or human kings. We might translate it "so-called gods," because the Psalmist is clearly referring to beings who are not actually divine. Jesus quoted verse 6: *I said, "You are gods; you are all sons of the Most High."* This is not a statement of their true identity, but rather of whom they claimed to be.

Jesus used the familiar rabbinical interpretive device that in Hebrew is called *qal wahomer,* meaning "light and heavy." This rule says that if something is true in a less important instance, then it is certainly true in a more important instance. Jesus made the point that if the Psalmist can refer to angels or human kings as "gods" when they clearly are not, how much more is it appropriate for him to make divine claims when it is absolutely his true identity and completely consistent with the life he has been living! Of course, they refused to accept even this biblical argument and tried to physically subdue Jesus, but for the third time he slipped away from a violent crowd. (See Luke 4:30 and John 8:59.)

How do you respond when someone challenges your theological assumptions or religious categories? Do you think you would have recognized Jesus' divinity if you were in the crowd that day? What can we learn from this challenging exchange?

REFLECT AND RESPOND

What is Jesus saying to me right now?

What step of faith is Jesus calling me to take today?

DAY 38

READ AND LISTEN: JOHN 11:1-16

Take a minute to listen for what God is saying in these verses…

COMMENT AND CONSIDER

Jesus was fully aware that the religious leaders in Jerusalem had decided to kill him. (See John 7:19-20.) He stayed in Galilee to keep clear of the authorities but ended up going to Jerusalem for the Festival of Shelters, first secretly and then, partway through the week, openly. (See John 7:1, 10, 14.) Once during that Festival, and again during the Festival of the Dedication, Jesus had to slip away from angry crowds that wanted to seize him and stone him to death. (See John 7:44; 8:20, 59; 10:31, 39.) To avoid arrest Jesus and his core disciples withdrew from Jerusalem and went into hiding on the east side of the Jordan River, near the place where John had been baptizing.

Their friends in Bethany, Mary and Martha, knew where they were, so when their brother Lazarus fell deathly ill, the sisters sent a messenger to tell Jesus, *"Lord, the one you love is sick."* Their implication was obvious; they were asking Jesus to come heal Lazarus. However, Jesus waited two days to respond to this urgent appeal. Some assume Jesus was waiting for Lazarus to die so he could raise him; however, that would be a cruel manipulation. No, if we count the days carefully, we find that Lazarus had already died by the time the messenger arrived. It took a full day for the messenger to travel to the Jordan River, Jesus waited two more days, then he spent the fourth day traveling back to Bethany. When he arrived, Jesus was told Lazarus had already been in the tomb four days. That means Lazarus must have died shortly after the messenger departed from Bethany.

Jesus waited two days so that people in Bethany would know he was really dead. First century Jews typically visited the tomb each of the first three days after a burial to make sure the person had not fallen into a coma and only seemed to have died. After the third day, it was confirmed the person was really dead. When Jesus said, *"Let's go to Judea again,"* the disciples reminded him there were crowds of people there who wanted to stone him to death. But Jesus said, *"If anyone walks during the day, he doesn't stumble, because he sees the light of this world."* Jesus lived in the confidence that doing what he saw the Father doing is how he would fulfill his purpose. (See John 5:19.) After two days the Father showed Jesus it was time to return to Bethany.

He told the disciples, *"Our friend Lazarus has fallen asleep, but I'm on my way to wake him up."* Sleep was a common metaphor for death among first-century Jews, and it is easy to understand why. When we die, we enter into a non-temporal state where we are no longer bound by the linear constraints of time. As Peter says, *With the Lord one day is like a thousand years, and a thousand years like one day.* (2 Peter 3:8) Sleep is the only time in this life we experience what it is like to be freed from the passage of time. We can fall asleep and wake up eight hours later but feel as if no time has passed.

Jesus said of those who die that he will *"raise them up on the last day."* (John 6:39) But he also told the repentant thief on the cross, *"Truly I tell you, today you will be with me in paradise."* (Luke 23:43) If death is like sleep and we are in that state where one day is like a thousand years, then even if we are raised a thousand years after our death, it will be as if no time has passed and we are awakening from a deep sleep into the fulness of God's Kingdom, reunited with all those who have died in Christ. Jesus is about to show them how to wake someone up from the sleep of death!

How do you feel about the inevitability of your physical death? How certain are you of the promise of eternal life? How does Jesus' description of death as sleep affect your view of death?

REFLECT AND RESPOND

What is Jesus saying to me right now?

What step of faith is Jesus calling me to take today?

DAY 39

READ AND LISTEN: JOHN 11:17-27

Take a minute to listen for what God is saying in these verses…

COMMENT AND CONSIDER

When people died in the ancient Middle East, the custom was to bury the body on the same day because decomposition began so quickly. In the Middle East, people honor those who have died with loud public expressions of grief. It was common to hire mourners to help express the grief of a family. These mourners typically gathered around the family tomb and home for the first week, wailing and lamenting loudly anytime people drew near. Musical instruments, such as flutes, accompanied these expressions of grief. Symbolic physical actions expressed grief as well, such as tearing clothing, heaping dust on the head, and sitting on the ground.

The first week following death was the most intense period of mourning. The family of the deceased stayed home, sitting on the floor wearing torn clothing, not bathing or cooking. Friends and neighbors would visit, bringing food and "sitting shiva" with them. This meant simply sitting with the family members and sharing their burden of grief. John describes these mourning customs when he says, *Many of the Jews had come to Martha and Mary to comfort them about their brother… Mary remained seated in the house.* When Martha heard Jesus had arrived, she got up from sitting shiva in the house and went out to meet him, but Mary remained behind.

Martha confronted Jesus by saying, *"Lord, if you had been here, my brother wouldn't have died."* This was both an indictment and a confession of faith. Martha was sure Jesus could have prevented her brother's death and was expressing the inevitable anger grief produces. The unspoken subtext of her statement was, "Why weren't you here? Why didn't you save him?" These questions flood the soul of everyone who loses someone they love. But Martha's statement was also an expression of her faith in Jesus. She truly believed he could have healed her brother. But the question remained: why didn't he?

This is often how we feel toward God when we lose a loved one. We know he could have healed them and angrily shake our fist at heaven because he didn't. But Martha doesn't let the grief trap her in this place of anger and blame. She takes the next step of faith by expressing audacious hope, *"Yet even now I know that whatever you ask from God, God will give you."* We have no way of knowing what Martha was thinking Jesus would do. Perhaps she didn't either. Maybe she just chose to trust Jesus even though it seemed there was no way out of this horrible pain and loss.

Jesus responded by saying, *"Your brother will rise again."* This sounded like the empty pious statements people use to try and short circuit our grief. Martha knew and believed in the doctrine of the resurrection of the dead at the end of time, but that didn't help her right now. Her heart was torn in two over the loss of her brother. It was him she wanted. Now. Jesus clarified by putting his promise in the present tense, *"I am the resurrection and the life. The one who believes in me, even if he dies, will live. Everyone who lives and believes in me will never die. Do you believe this?"* Jesus was not offering an abstract theological doctrine but was offering himself. He was inviting her to put her broken heart in his hands and to leave the rest to him.

Martha accepted his invitation. *"Yes, Lord,"* she told him, *"I believe you are the Messiah, the Son of God, who comes into the world."* She didn't know what would happen, but she knew she could trust Jesus. His presence and promise were enough for her. How do you process your grief? Are you able to honestly tell Jesus how you feel, even if it includes anger and blame directed at him? What does it mean for you to trust Jesus more than a doctrine or an outcome?

REFLECT AND RESPOND

What is Jesus saying to me right now?

What step of faith is Jesus calling me to take today?

DAY 40

READ AND LISTEN: JOHN 11:28-44

Take a minute to listen for what God is saying in these verses…

COMMENT AND CONSIDER

For the past four days, Mary and Martha had been "sitting shiva" with their extended family in the home they shared together, mourning the death of their brother. Friends and neighbors came by with food to sit with them in their grief. When word came to them that Jesus was on the outskirts of the village, Martha immediately went to him, but Mary didn't move. In her anger she refused to honor Jesus by going out to greet him.

After their conversation, Jesus asked Martha where Mary was. Embarrassed that her sister was dishonoring Jesus in this way, Martha hurried back to the house to get her. Jesus waited just outside the village, keeping a low profile due to the political threats against him. This is why it was in private that Martha pulled Mary aside to tell her, *"The Teacher is here and is calling for you."* This news broke Mary's resolve, and she ran out of the house to Jesus.

When Mary came to him, she fell down at his feet, weeping. Disciples sat at the feet of their rabbi, and Mary once again took the posture of a disciple. (See Luke 10:38-42.) Through her tears she repeated the same indicting and faith-filled statement her sister had used, *"Lord, if you had been here, my brother wouldn't have died!"* While Martha's more practical tone had evoked a theological conversation about resurrection, Mary's more passionate tone moved Jesus emotionally.

John, an eyewitness to this interaction, uses very evocative words to describe Jesus' reaction: *he was deeply moved in his spirit and troubled.* Both these Greek words express the gut-level anger and pain genuine grief causes when we lose someone close. As they made their way to the tomb, Jesus began to weep with Mary. Those watching said, *"See how he loved him!"* But they misunderstood Jesus' tears. Jesus knew he was going to raise Lazarus from the dead, so he wasn't weeping over Lazarus. (See John 11:11.) He was weeping over the pain of those who grieved Lazarus' death. Compassion is the willingness to share the pain of others to lighten the burden and isolation of their grief. Jesus chooses to enter the pain of those who are suffering and weep with them.

Those who could afford it had rock-cut tombs built for their extended families. The body was anointed with scented oil, covered with a shroud, and carefully wrapped in strips of linen, with a separate piece over the face. The body was then placed on a rock shelf or in a slot cut into the wall of the tomb. The outer door of the tomb was sealed with a stone plug that fit into the opening or a cylindrical stone that rolled in a sloped track, covering the entrance. Either way, the door was sealed with clay to contain the smell of the decomposing body. Then, a year later, the family opened the tomb to gather the bones into a stone bone box called an ossuary.

When they arrived at the family tomb, Jesus said the very last thing anyone expected, *"Remove the stone."* Martha, always the practical one, objected, pointing out the smell of the decaying body would be overpowering. But Jesus challenged Martha to simply trust him. Then, after a prayer to the Father, Jesus exercised the authority given to him as Son of the King and commanded, *"Lazarus, come out!"* And to everyone's shock and amazement, the still-bound Lazarus stumbled out of the darkness of death into the blinding light of life! Jesus instructed his disciples to remove the grave cloths so Lazarus could step back into the freedom of his restored life. It was the seventh and greatest of Jesus' signs as recorded by John. It is indisputable proof that Jesus has the power to transform death into life.

What does it mean to you that Jesus is willing to enter your pain and weep with you? How does that move you to become a more compassionate person to those around you? What are the implications of Jesus' authority over death for your life today? Are there people in your life whom Jesus is calling you to *"unbind"*?

REFLECT AND RESPOND

What is Jesus saying to me right now?

What step of faith is Jesus calling me to take today?

DAY 41

READ AND LISTEN: JOHN 11:45-57

Take a minute to listen for what God is saying in these verses…

COMMENT AND CONSIDER

Jesus' raising of Lazarus proved to be a turning point in his mission. Lazarus' testimony was a powerful affirmation of Jesus' legitimacy and power. The people of Bethany saw Lazarus' body carried through the village and sealed in the tomb. After four days they knew that he really was dead. But then many eyewitnesses watched as Jesus called him back to life and out of the tomb. And there he was, walking around, telling everyone what Jesus had done for him. It is hard to imagine a more compelling witness than that! As John says, *Therefore, many of the Jews who came to Mary and saw what he did believed in him.* Faith in Jesus was growing among the people. But, as we have seen throughout Jesus' mission, for every authoritative teaching and powerful miracle Jesus performed, there seemed to be an opposite reaction of fear and reprisal from those in power who were threatened by his authority. When word got back to the Pharisees of what Jesus had done in Bethany, they went to the chief priests who convened a meeting of the Sanhedrin to discuss how to shut Jesus down.

The Sanhedrin was the ruling council of 70 in Jerusalem who oversaw religious and civic matters for the Jewish community. Led by the High Priest, the council was comprised of leaders from the priestly aristocracy of Jerusalem, wealthy lay families from the city, Pharisees, and other experts in the Law. They met in the Chamber of Hewn Stone, one of the rooms surrounding the innermost courts of the Temple, and had a militia of Temple Police who enforced their rulings. While Rome gave them authority over the religious and civic affairs of the Jewish community, they were not given power to impose the death penalty. Only the Roman governor, who also appointed the High Priests, could impose a death sentence.

John takes us into the Chamber of Hewn Stone to listen in on the discussion the members of the Sanhedrin were having about Jesus. Perhaps Nicodemus and Joseph of Arimathea reported this to John after the resurrection. Considering Jesus' raising of Lazarus, they said, *"If we let him go on like this, everyone will believe in him, and the Romans will come and take away both our place and our nation."* The primary way these Jewish leaders retained their power was by keeping the peace and cooperating with the Romans. Caiaphas was the longest reigning High Priest in the entire first century, testimony of his ability to work with these pagan overlords. He stood up and said, *"You know nothing at all! You're not considering that it is to your advantage that one man should die for the people rather than the whole nation perish."*

Little did Caiaphas know that his statement of political expediency was pointing to a deeper, prophetic truth about Jesus' impending death. Jesus would indeed *die for the people*, but not to keep Caiaphas in power (he was deposed in AD 36); rather, to save the whole world. As John explains, the High Priest's words were an unconscious prophecy that *Jesus was going to die for the nation, and not for the nation only, but also to unite the scattered children of God.* Sometimes we are part of something bigger than ourselves without realizing it. Caiaphas was so focused on his own power and purposes that he couldn't see what God was really doing in Jesus. Nicodemus and Joseph of Arimathea, on the other hand, recognized the day of the visitation in Jesus and ultimately chose God's Kingdom over their own. (See John 19:38-42.)

Although not many of us have a testimony as dramatic as Lazarus, we all have a story to tell. What is your testimony of what Jesus has done in your life? Are you ready and willing to tell others? How can you recognize what God is doing in your context so that you can be part of it rather than working against it?

REFLECT AND RESPOND

What is Jesus saying to me right now?

What step of faith is Jesus calling me to take today?

DAY 42

READ AND LISTEN: JOHN 12:1-11

Take a minute to listen for what God is saying in these verses…

COMMENT AND CONSIDER

Knowing the Sanhedrin planned to arrest him and have him executed, Jesus withdrew into hiding in Ephraim, about 20 miles north of Jerusalem. As pilgrims began to gather in Jerusalem for the Passover, they speculated that Jesus wouldn't come given the threats of the authorities. (See John 11:56.) But Jesus did come, with his core male and female disciples, joining the throngs of pilgrims making their way from Jericho to Jerusalem. But before Jesus made his triumphal entry over the Mount of Olives into the Holy City, he and his disciples arrived in Bethany about a week before the Passover celebrations were to begin.

Bethany was a village about a mile and a half east of Jerusalem on the opposite slope of the Mount of Olives. After resting on the Sabbath there in the family home of his close friends Mary, Martha, and Lazarus, Jesus attended a special banquet in his honor hosted by a man known as *Simon the Leper*. (See Matthew 26:6; Mark 14:3.) Lepers were forbidden to even come close to others, so Simon must have been one of the many "used-to-bes" among Jesus' followers. There were people who used to be blind, used to be demonized, used to be tax collectors, used to be prostitutes. Simon used to be a leper, but Jesus had healed him, and he wanted to thank Jesus by throwing a party in his honor. He also invited Lazarus who used to be dead!

Jews normally ate their meals sitting upright, but for banquets they followed the Greek and Roman custom of reclining on cushions around a low, three-sided table called a *triclinium*. At a public banquet, only men would recline around the table. The women prepared and served the meal. Predictably Martha helped the other women serve, while Lazarus reclined at the table with Simon, Jesus, and the other invited male guests. Mary, however, had other plans.

Earlier in Galilee a woman, known in her community as a "sinner," entered a similar banquet given in Jesus' honor, anointing his feet with perfume and her tears, drying his feet with her hair. (See Luke 7:36-50.) This is clearly a different event, and yet there are so many similarities it seems Mary heard about that dramatic anointing and decided she would do something similar to honor her rabbi. To everyone's surprise, she entered the dining room, knelt where Jesus was reclining with his feet extended away from the table, poured out a lavish amount of perfumed oil on his feet, and let down her hair to wipe away the excess oil.

The host of a banquet normally made a foot-washing basin available to his guests upon their arrival, perhaps with a slave to wash their feet for them. At a fancy banquet, the host sometimes offered guests refreshing oil to rub on their hair and beard as we often experience in our travels in the Middle East still today. The fact that Mary entered this all-male banquet was radically counter-cultural. Anointing Jesus' feet was a shocking act of lavish and humble devotion. Letting her hair down to wipe his feet would have raised some eyebrows among the religiously conservative, as women were meant to keep their hair modestly covered in public.

Magnifying Mary's dramatic act of devotion was the value of this oil scented with the rare spikenard plant, originating from Northern India. Normally this kind of expensive oil came in very small vials, sealed to contain the scent. But Mary poured out an entire pint of the oil, a huge amount valued at nearly a year's salary! Some have speculated this was so costly it may have been part of Mary's dowry and represented a significant part of her financial security. When Judas, the embezzler, criticized this lavish act of devotion, Jesus defended her, interpreting her actions as a prophetic act anticipating the anointing of his soon-to-be dead body.

What limits your expression of love and devotion to Jesus? Are you afraid of what others might think of you? Do you hold back because of cultural expectations? What price are you willing to pay to publicly express your love for Jesus?

REFLECT AND RESPOND

What is Jesus saying to me right now?

What step of faith is Jesus calling me to take today?

FOOTSTEPS EVERY WEEK: REVIEW

Write a brief summary of what Jesus said to you each day this past week and the step of faith he called you to take:

MONDAY

TUESDAY

WEDNESDAY

THURSDAY

FRIDAY

SATURDAY

Footsteps Every Week: Reflect

Big Picture

As you look over what Jesus has said to you this past week, do you see any themes? What is the most important thing you need to remember and believe?

Predictable Pattern

As you look over what Jesus called you to do this past week, is there a new predictable pattern he is inviting you to establish in your life with God and others?

Plant the Word

As you look over the readings from this past week, write out the passage that feels most important for you and memorize it over the next week:

DAY 43

READ AND LISTEN: JOHN 12:12-19

Take a minute to listen for what God is saying in these verses…

COMMENT AND CONSIDER

Jews traveled to Jerusalem for the major festivals from all around the Mediterranean world, as well as from across the Fertile Crescent. Passover was by far the most popular holiday and drew the largest crowds. As pilgrims began their final ascent up the Judean hills toward Jerusalem, they sang the "Songs of Ascent" (Psalms 120-134). As they drew near to the Holy City itself, the excitement grew even more intense, and they sang the "Hallel Songs" (Psalms 113-118). Pilgrims coming from the Jordan Valley in the east passed through Jericho with its huge date palm plantations. This was a natural place for them to cut palm branches to wave like pom-poms in joyful celebration during the final leg of their journey.

From the very beginning of his mission, the authority of Jesus' words and the power of his actions constantly evoked the question: who is this man? Many rumors circulated about his identity: John the Baptist come back from the dead, Elijah returned from heaven on his fiery chariot, the great Prophet promised to Moses. (See Matthew 16:13-16.) But Jesus consistently dodged questions of his identity because he didn't want the religious authorities to cut his mission short by arresting him before he could fulfill everything the Father had sent him to do. His more recent teaching in the Temple Courts and his raising of Lazarus pointed people to his divine nature, which is why he had to go into hiding from the authorities. But now he was ready to reveal his true identity.

The Synoptic Gospels tell us Jesus made special arrangements to borrow a young donkey to make his dramatic entrance from Bethany, over the Mount of Olives, into Jerusalem. (See Matthew 21:1-3.) This act was filled with prophetic meaning since Zechariah specifically prophesied the Messiah would enter Jerusalem from the Mount of Olives riding a young donkey. (See Zechariah 9:9, 14:4.) Jesus was boldly declaring his Messianic identity for everyone to see. The crowds immediately understood what he was doing when they saw him ride that young donkey over the Mount of Olives, and they began to chant the line from one of the Hallel Psalms: *"Hosanna! Blessed is he who comes in the name of the Lord..."* To be crystal clear about what this meant, they added their own declaration, *"the King of Israel!"*

There was no doubt in anyone's mind who Jesus was claiming to be. The Messiah is the divinely anointed King, descended from David to fulfill the promise of an eternal Kingdom that will never end. The crowds whipped themselves into a frenzy, thinking Jesus was coming as a military conqueror who was going to destroy the Romans and set up his own government. They didn't notice Jesus was riding a donkey instead of a war horse. They didn't listen to how Jesus defined his own Kingdom. Not even his closest disciples understood the nature of his mission, even though he told them repeatedly he was coming to Jerusalem to die. Jesus is the promised King but came as the Prince of Peace to lay down his life in order to establish a spiritual Kingdom that will last forever.

It is with a certain amount of irony that John records the Pharisees' lament: *"You see? You've accomplished nothing. Look, the world has gone after him!"* Little did they know that the Temple would soon be destroyed, all Jews would be banished from Jerusalem, and the movement of Jesus would spread to the very ends of the earth! But at the time, neither John nor any of the disciples were able to comprehend what was unfolding before their eyes. It wasn't until after Jesus' death and resurrection and the outpouring of the Holy Spirit that everything started to make sense to them.

What does it mean for you to recognize Jesus as your true King? What presuppositions do you need to let go of to enter more fully into his Kingdom? How can you gain a clearer perspective as you look back and consider how Jesus has worked in your life?

REFLECT AND RESPOND

What is Jesus saying to me right now?

What step of faith is Jesus calling me to take today?

DAY 44

READ AND LISTEN: JOHN 12:20-36

Take a minute to listen for what God is saying in these verses…

COMMENT AND CONSIDER

During Jesus' final Passover week, he and his closest disciples stayed in Bethany with the family of Mary, Martha, and Lazarus. Each morning they walked the mile and a half over the Mount of Olives, through the Kidron Valley, and up into the Temple Courts. The crowds who gathered in the enormous courtyard of the Temple grew each day as the Passover drew near. The religious authorities were too afraid of the crowd's reaction to openly arrest Jesus, but they listened to his teaching and tried to trap him with trick questions to find a plausible pretense to arrest him. But Jesus evaded all their efforts.

From the very beginning of his public mission, Jesus was clear that the Good News of the Kingdom was for every person, every tribe, and every nation. This is why they tried to stone him in Nazareth. (See Luke 4:16-30.) Yet his missional strategy in Galilee was to focus on *the lost sheep of the house of Israel.* (Matthew 10:6) Jesus didn't reject the Gentiles; he just chose to direct his message to the Jewish peasants of Galilee. But along the way, he healed the centurion's servant, the Syrophoenician woman's daughter, delivered the Gerasene demoniac of a legion of demons, and gave the Samaritan woman living water that changed her whole town. (See Matthew 8:5-13, Mark 7:24-30, Luke 8:26-39, and John 4:4-26.)

A growing number of Gentiles were curious about Judaism, and many had come to believe in the God of the Bible. Most were not ready to fully convert by taking on all the ceremonial laws of Judaism, particularly circumcision, but they worshiped in the synagogue, studied the Torah, and prayed to the God of Israel. These people were called "God-fearers." The Greeks who came to Jerusalem for Passover and asked to see Jesus were most likely from among these believing Gentiles. Perhaps they had heard about Jesus from the formerly demonized man whom Jesus sent into the Greek cities of the Decapolis to the east of the Sea of Galilee. (See Luke 8:39.)

It is no accident these Greek believers asking to see Jesus approached Philip. He was the only member of Jesus' inner circle of disciples with a Greek name. He lived in Bethsaida, which recent archaeological discoveries have confirmed was a Jewish fishing town on the north shore of the Sea of Galilee, just east of the place where the Jordan River flows into the lake. This was in Herod Philip's territory, who was the ruler most aligned with Greek culture and religion. His territory was adjacent to the region of the Greek cities of the Decapolis. It is likely Philip spoke Greek as his primary language.

When Philip told Andrew about them, they both decided to tell Jesus, but Jesus responded by speaking of his impending death. *"The hour has come for the Son of Man to be glorified. Truly I tell you, unless a grain of wheat falls to the ground and dies, it remains by itself. But if it dies, it produces much fruit."* Jesus knew his time to focus on the lost sheep of the house of Israel was coming to an end and the universal mission which would take the Apostles to the ends of the earth was about to begin. He knew that carrying out this mission to the world meant that the disciples would face persecution, suffering, and even death for the sake of the Gospel. And so he promised them, *"The one who loves his life will lose it, and the one who hates his life in this world will keep it for eternal life."* Jesus knew his own death would open the door for this Good News to reach every tribe and nation on the planet. *"As for me, if I am lifted up from the earth I will draw all people to myself."*

How big is your missional target? Do you have a bullseye that you are focusing on as Jesus did? What are you willing to sacrifice to reach those who are lost? How is Jesus calling you to lay down your life in order to fulfill your mission?

REFLECT AND RESPOND

What is Jesus saying to me right now?

What step of faith is Jesus calling me to take today?

DAY 45

READ AND LISTEN: JOHN 12:37-50

Take a minute to listen for what God is saying in these verses…

COMMENT AND CONSIDER

It is easy to assume the eyewitnesses of Jesus' teaching and miracles had an easier time believing. However, most who heard Jesus and saw his miracles firsthand did not trust him enough to follow. The three towns in Galilee where Jesus spent the most time and performed the most miracles— Capernaum, Chorazin, and Bethsaida—were also the most resistant to his message. (See Luke 10:13-16.) John points to the mystery of disbelief by quoting Isaiah, *"He has blinded their eyes and hardened their hearts, so that they would not see with their eyes or understand with their hearts, and turn, and I would heal them."* (See Isaiah 6:10.)

This is a hard passage to understand. At first it seems Jesus is saying God purposefully causes certain people not to believe by blinding their eyes and hardening their hearts. But Jesus already clearly stated that he came for everyone. *"For God loved the world in this way: He gave his one and only Son, so that everyone who believes in him will not perish but have eternal life. For God did not send his Son into the world to condemn the world, but to save the world through him."* God loves the whole world (Greek: *cosmos*), and it was for the whole world that Jesus came. Jesus never turned anyone away, even his enemies. Jesus said, *If anyone hears my words and doesn't keep them, I do not judge him; for I did not come to judge the world but to save the world.*

Isaiah's language echoes the description of what happened during the Exodus when God used plagues to pressure Pharaoh into letting the people of Israel go. Four times the text says that Pharaoh *hardened his heart* (See Exodus 8:15, 8:32, 9:12, and 9:34). But in the same narrative, four times God says, *"I will harden Pharaoh's heart"* (See Exodus 4:21, 7:3, 10:1, and 14:4). So which is it, God or Pharaoh? The picture we get is of God applying pressure to the will of Pharaoh, and Pharaoh resisting God's will. As that pressure increased, Pharaoh's heart was hardened, like steel between the hammer and the anvil. Was it God or Pharaoh doing the hardening? Both.

Jesus confronts people with a decision. Will we receive Jesus' message, embrace him as our Savior, and follow him as our King? Or will we reject his words, deny his identity, and go our own way? The more we resist submission and stubbornly hold on to control in our lives, the more the call of Jesus presses against our heart. As we persist in our resistance, our heart is hardened, our eyes are blinded, and our understanding is clouded. Is it us or God doing this? Both. But, as Paul says, *"whenever a person turns to the Lord, the veil is removed."* (2 Corinthians 3:16)

Often Jesus concluded his teaching by saying, *"Let anyone who has ears to hear listen."* (See Mark 4:9, 23; Luke 8:8, 14:35.) He is asking if we are willing to receive what he is saying and respond by exercising the faith his Word creates. Jesus does not reject or condemn anyone. But anyone who refuses to accept the truth is condemned by that very truth. Jesus simply said what the Father told him to say. How we respond to that Word determines our destiny. As Jesus said, *"The one who rejects me and doesn't receive my sayings has this as his judge: The word I have spoken will judge him on the last day."*

God's love is universal and unconditional, freely offered to every person on the planet. But God will not force us to love him back and follow Jesus. The question is whether we will receive the love his Spirit is pouring into our hearts and exercise the faith his Word is producing in us. (See Romans 5:5; 10:17.) If we resist the Spirit, reject his love, and deny his truth, then our hearts will be hardened and our eyes will be blinded. Are there any ways you are resisting the Spirit? Rejecting his love? Denying his truth? How can you let Jesus soften your heart and open your eyes today?

REFLECT AND RESPOND

What is Jesus saying to me right now?

What step of faith is Jesus calling me to take today?

DAY 46

READ AND LISTEN: JOHN 13:1-17

Take a minute to listen for what God is saying in these verses…

COMMENT AND CONSIDER

Archaeology and history point to a large house on the wealthy southwest hill as the place Jesus arranged to share his final Passover meal with the disciples. It probably belonged to the extended family of Mary, the mother of John Mark and the cousin of Barnabas. Jesus sent Peter and John to prepare the meal in a large upper room of that home. (See Luke 22:7-13.) The Synoptic Gospels specify this was a celebration of the Passover, but John tells us it happened on the night before Passover eve. (See John 19:14, 42.) It is likely Jesus chose to celebrate the Passover one day early because he knew the authorities were about to arrest him and wanted to make sure nothing interfered with this final meal.

Once Jesus and the disciples were reclining around a low three-sided table in that upper room, he did something none of them could have anticipated. He stood up, took off his outer cloak, wrapped a towel around his waist, and began washing each of the disciples' feet. This was outrageous and unthinkable! Very few first-century homes had indoor toilets or sewers, so chamber pots were typically used, and the refuse was often dumped into the streets. Add to that the manure of animals and the general accumulation of food waste, and it's clear that ancient streets could be a nasty place indeed.

It is not surprising that sandal-clad feet were seen as the most unclean part of the body and considered untouchable in that culture. It also makes sense that washing your feet was a welcome act before entering a banquet. Hospitable hosts often made water available to their guests in a special basin that featured a small post in the middle on which to rest your heel while washing your feet. In a wealthy home, the lowest slave was often provided to wash the feet of the guests as they arrived. It was such a reviled task that later rabbis exempted Jewish slaves from this role.

The disciples were reclining with their feet extended away from the table, so Jesus made his way around their perimeter, washing and drying their feet. When he came to Peter at the far end of the table, Peter refused to let Jesus wash his feet. In an honor/shame culture, it was too shameful for Peter to allow his esteemed Rabbi to take on this lowest of servile roles. In the Mishnah we read that Rabbi Gamaliel mixed a cup of water and wine for Rabbi Eliezer, but Eliezer was unwilling to accept this act of service from the more senior rabbi. Jesus washing Peter's feet was a far greater reversal of roles in that culture.

Jesus expressed how this reversal of cultural hierarchies is at the core of his Kingdom when he told Peter, *"If I don't wash you, you have no part with me."* There is no other way to be part of Jesus' family and Kingdom except by receiving his self-giving service and love. In this shameful act of service, Jesus foreshadowed the ultimate shameful sacrifice he would endure on our behalf by submitting to death on a cross.

Peter predictably swung to the opposite extreme, *"Lord, not only my feet, but also my hands and my head."* But Jesus made it clear that this foot washing was not like the ritual baths they had taken to purify themselves before the Passover, nor was it like the symbolic handwashing that was part of the meal. Jesus' act of humble service was a clear example of how they were to serve one another and lead others. *"So if I, your Lord and Teacher, have washed your feet, you also ought to wash one another's feet. For I have given you an example, that you also should do just as I have done for you."* Using the *qal wahomer* principle (Hebrew for "light and heavy"), Jesus pointed out that if he as Teacher and Lord had done this for them, how much more were they to humble themselves as servant leaders?

Are you willing to receive Jesus' humble, self-giving service? How can his gift of grace empower you to humble yourself and serve others in love?

REFLECT AND RESPOND

What is Jesus saying to me right now?

What step of faith is Jesus calling me to take today?

DAY 47

READ AND LISTEN: JOHN 13:18-30

Take a minute to listen for what God is saying in these verses…

COMMENT AND CONSIDER

In the first century, people ate special meals reclining on couches or pillows around a three-sided table, leaning on their left elbow and eating with their right hand. The seating order was determined by the level of honor assigned to each participant. The host normally reclined in the second to the last spot on the left side of the U-shaped table (if you are facing the open end). To his right was either his wife, if it was a family meal, or a co-host if a mixed group of male guests. To his left was the guest of honor. A descending degree of honor was assigned to each person who sat further from the host. The position of lowest honor was at the end of the "U" on the right side, across the table from the host.

During the meal Jesus told his disciples the shocking news one of them would betray him. John tells us, *One of his disciples, the one Jesus loved, was reclining close beside Jesus.* Most likely this was John, son of Zebedee and author of the Gospel. While leaning on his left elbow, John was able to lean back against Jesus, which means he was seated to the right of Jesus in the honorific co-host position. Peter had to motion across the table for John to ask Jesus who the betrayer was, which means he was seated in one of the lowest positions of honor. Jesus told John, *"He's the one I give the piece of bread to after I have dipped it."* Then Judas Iscariot dipped into the bowl with Jesus. This means Judas was seated to the left of Jesus in the place of highest honor.

Earlier Jesus had taught his disciples, *"Don't sit in the place of honor… But when you are invited, go and sit in the lowest place, so that when the one who invited you comes, he will say to you, 'Friend, move up higher.' You will then be honored…"* (Luke 14:8-10) Perhaps Peter had this in mind and took the place of lowest honor, hoping to be invited up to a higher position. However, Jesus gave Judas the place of special honor, a shocking act of grace given what Judas was about to do. Perhaps Jesus was inviting Judas to choose a different course even at the final hour.

Sadly, even this gracious invitation to the place of honor was not enough to change Judas' mind. After receiving the bread from Jesus, Judas abruptly left the gathering to tell the authorities where they could find Jesus. Throughout history many have speculated why one of Jesus' closest disciples, who had heard his incredible teaching and witnessed his indisputable miracles, would choose to betray his master. Many assume Judas was driven by the devil from the beginning, but it seems unlikely Jesus would have invited someone under the spell of evil into his inner circle and entrusted the finances to him. John tells us it was at the very end when Judas fell under the power of the devil. (See also Luke 22:3.)

Others have speculated Judas was so disappointed Jesus didn't take up the mantle of a military messiah, ready to lead his followers into battle against the Romans, and that he simply gave up on his rabbi. But this doesn't adequately explain the depth of Judas' remorse after Jesus' arrest. (See Matthew 27:3-5.) I am sure Judas was disappointed Jesus took the path of non-violence, repeatedly telling them he was going to lay down his life, but I think Judas still thought if push came to shove and Jesus was backed into a corner, he would come out fighting. Perhaps Judas believed that if he put Jesus into that corner, he would force Jesus' hand and provoke him to become the messiah he wanted him to be.

In what ways does the real Jesus not fit your expectations of him? Are you ever disappointed that Jesus isn't doing what you want him to do? In what ways is the devil trying to get you to fashion your own messiah who fits your plans and desires?

REFLECT AND RESPOND

What is Jesus saying to me right now?

What step of faith is Jesus calling me to take today?

DAY 48

READ AND LISTEN: JOHN 13:31-38

Take a minute to listen for what God is saying in these verses…

COMMENT AND CONSIDER

After Judas left the upper room to inform the religious authorities of Jesus' whereabouts, Jesus knew the die was cast. He said, *"Now the Son of Man is glorified, and God is glorified in him."* He knew the events had been set in motion that would result in unimaginable suffering but also the completion of his mission to the glory of his Father. He prepared the disciples by explaining, *"Little children, I am with you a little while longer. You will look for me, and just as I told the Jews, so now I tell you, 'Where I am going, you cannot come.'"*

The poignant intimacy of this final evening together is expressed in Jesus' address *"little children."* As their rabbi, Jesus had become a spiritual father to them, which meant they were brothers and sisters to one another, a spiritual family living on mission together. To help guide them through the tumultuous days and years ahead, Jesus gave them a new commandment, *"Love one another. Just as I have loved you, you are also to love one another. By this everyone will know that you are my disciples, if you love one another."*

The Greek verb *phileo* describes the affectionate love between friends, the verb *erao* communicates the passionate love between lovers, and the verb *stergo* expresses the familial love between a parent and child. But here John uses the Greek verb *agapao* to express Jesus' command to love one another with an unconditional, self-giving love that sacrificially seeks what is best for the other. This kind of unselfish, giving love is to define the relationships between the members of the spiritual family Jesus formed.

Jesus gave them a clear example of the kind of self-giving relationships of love he was talking about: *"Just as I have loved you, you are also to love one another."* The unconditional love Jesus showed them was to be the model of their love for one another. Disciples intentionally imitated the life of their rabbi. Jesus told them to imitate the self-giving love they had received from him and watched him give to so many. This was to shape the way they would live as a spiritual family on mission in the years to come.

The hyper-religious Essenes at Qumran were exhorted to love one another but hate those outside their exclusive community. By contrast Jesus had already taught his disciples to love God with their whole being and to love their neighbor as themselves. (See Mark 12:29-31.) Jesus was clear that their love for each other would overflow from their spiritual family to touch the lives of those who watched their way of life: *"By this everyone will know that you are my disciples, if you love one another."* This kind of Jesus-shaped love became the defining characteristic of the followers of Jesus and was a key to their massively disproportionate impact on the Roman Empire. Just over a hundred years later, during the devastating Antonine Plague which killed about 10 percent of the population, the courageous, unconditional love of the followers of Jesus who cared for the sick and dying impacted the world's perspective on Jesus and the Kingdom he offered.

The love Jesus poured into the disciples was to define their relationships with each other and empower them to love in this self-giving way. In turn, living out this kind of love for one another in spiritual family was to impact the lost and overflow into the broken lives of the hurting, bringing hope and life to the world. Later, John explained it this way to the many spiritual families he oversaw in Asia Minor: *"Love consists in this: not that we loved God, but that he loved us and sent his Son to be the atoning sacrifice for our sins. Dear friends, if God loved us in this way, we also must love one another."* (1 John 4:10-11)

What defines your relationship with other disciples? How can Jesus' self-giving love empower you to love others in the same way? How can you show this love to the lost and hurting?

REFLECT AND RESPOND

What is Jesus saying to me right now?

What step of faith is Jesus calling me to take today?

FOOTSTEPS EVERY WEEK: REVIEW

Write a brief summary of what Jesus said to you each day this past week and the step of faith he called you to take:

MONDAY

TUESDAY

WEDNESDAY

THURSDAY

FRIDAY

SATURDAY

FOOTSTEPS EVERY WEEK: REFLECT

BIG PICTURE

As you look over what Jesus has said to you this past week, do you see any themes? What is the most important thing you need to remember and believe?

PREDICTABLE PATTERN

As you look over what Jesus called you to do this past week, is there a new predictable pattern he is inviting you to establish in your life with God and others?

PLANT THE WORD

As you look over the readings from this past week, write out the passage that feels most important for you and memorize it over the next week:

DAY 49

READ AND LISTEN: JOHN 14:1-14

Take a minute to listen for what God is saying in these verses…

COMMENT AND CONSIDER

Jesus' statements about going away filled the disciples with confusion and fear. He reassured them: *"Don't let your heart be troubled. Believe in God; believe also in me."* The Greek word translated "believe" here is *pisteuo,* which is the verbal form of faith meaning exercise faith by putting your trust in me. His word plants faith in our hearts, and we are called to exercise that faith by taking concrete steps, following in his footsteps by the power of the Spirit. We may not understand what he is doing or where he is going, but every day the question is whether we are trusting Jesus enough to follow him.

To reassure his disciples, Jesus gave them a powerful promise, *"In my Father's house are many rooms. If it were not so, would I have told you that I am going to prepare a place for you?"* In biblical times people lived as extended families in houses with multiple rooms arranged around a central courtyard. Each room housed a nuclear family or several single people. The Greek word for this kind of family and home is *oikos,* the word John uses for *house* in verse 2. When a bridegroom was engaged to a bride, he began to build a new room onto the *oikos* house to prepare their place in the extended family. When the wedding took place, the groom went to the family home of the bride to bring her to their new home with their new family.

Jesus told his disciples he is the bridegroom who is going away for a time to prepare our place in the Father's great family. When he returns, he will bring us home as his bride into our eternal family where we belong forever. However, we don't have to wait until the end of history to find our place in that family. Jesus showed his disciples how to build an extended spiritual family living on mission together here and now.

Thomas asked, *"Lord, we don't know where you're going. How can we know the way?"* They had followed Jesus for the past three years, but now Jesus told them he was going somewhere they couldn't come. How would they find their way into that eternal family? Jesus answered by pointing to himself: *"I am the way, the truth, and the life. No one comes to the Father except through me."* Only by trusting Jesus and following him will we find our way into that family.

Often, we focus on studying the truth of Jesus, which is right because his truth sets us free. (See John 8:32.) Sometimes we aspire to the life of Jesus but are intimidated because we don't feel we can live a life like his. But most of the time, we overlook the *way* of Jesus: the intentional patterns to his life, rhythms he kept, groups he gathered, and methods he used. The call to "follow me" is an invitation to imitate the *way* of Jesus so our life begins to look more and more like his. In following the way of Jesus and trusting the truth of Jesus, we will be empowered to live the kind of life Jesus lived: The WAY + The TRUTH = The LIFE! This is how we take up our place today in God's great, eternal family.

Jesus made his divinity clear when he told Philip, *"The one who has seen me has seen the Father."* But he also told the disciples that *"the one who believes in me will also do the works that I do. And he will do even greater works than these, because I am going to the Father."* Although Jesus was going away physically, he would soon send his Spirit to fill them. (See John 14:15-17.) As his disciples learned to walk in his way and trust his truth, they would do the same things Jesus did, even the supernatural things! The same is true for us today.

How is Jesus calling you to trust him right now? How can you learn to recognize and follow his way? Do you believe you can learn to do everything Jesus did?

REFLECT AND RESPOND

What is Jesus saying to me right now?

What step of faith is Jesus calling me to take today?

DAY 50

READ AND LISTEN: JOHN 14:15-26

Take a minute to listen for what God is saying in these verses…

COMMENT AND CONSIDER

The story of the Bible is the story of God's love for us. God created us in his image as his beloved children. (See Genesis 1:27.) God is good, and his love for us is complete. (See Jeremiah 31:3.) His invitation is for us to love him in return. Jesus said the most important thing in life is to return God's love: *"Love the Lord your God with all your heart, with all your soul, with all your mind, and with all your strength."* (Mark 12:30) God's commands are an expression of his love for us. Since God is all-good and all-knowing, not only does he want what is best for us, but he knows what is best for us. His desire is for us to flourish, bear good fruit that lasts, and fulfill our purpose. Loving God and doing his will is the path to that fulfillment.

This is why God so often tells us about the inherent connection between loving him and doing his will. He repeatedly promises his love and blessing to *"those who love me and keep my commands."* (Exodus 20:6. See Deuteronomy 5:10, 7:9; 11:1, 13, 22; 30:16; Joshua 22:5; Nehemiah 1:5; Psalm 119:47-48; 119:127; Daniel 9:4.) So it is not surprising Jesus made the same connection, *"If you love me, you will keep my commands."* If we love God, we will trust his love for us. If we trust him, we will recognize the goodness of his will. If we recognize how good his will is, we will seek to do it. Years later John summed it up this way: *"this is what love for God is: to keep his commands."* (1 John 5:3)

It seems so simple and clear, except that we are broken people who live in a fallen world. Our flesh is that part of us still in bondage to sin, and we have an enemy of our soul who seeks to steal, kill, and destroy what is good. As a result, Paul tells us, *"the desire to do what is good is with me, but there is no ability to do it. For I do not do the good that I want to do, but I practice the evil that I do not want to do."* (Romans 7:18-19) This is why, even when we love God, we so often fail to do his will.

But Jesus has not left us alone. We are not orphans. Even though Jesus was going away physically, he was about to ask the Father to send the Spirit to fill us with God's presence. Jesus says the Spirit is *"another Counselor."* John uses the Greek word *paracletos,* which can be translated "Counselor," "Advocate," "Comforter," "Intercessor," or "Helper." The Paraclete comes alongside to help us, fight for us, guide us, and empower us. In the Old Testament, we read of the Spirit of God occasionally coming upon prophets and kings, empowering them to do God's will in extraordinary circumstances. But now, Jesus says, the Spirit *"remains with you and will be in you."*

The closer Jesus drew to the final fulfillment of his mission, the more explicitly he explained his true identity. In the upper room, Jesus gave his disciples the full revelation of God as Father, Son, and Holy Spirit. Jesus told them he and the Father are one. Although he was going away, the Holy Spirit would soon come and fill them. Jesus said, *"On that day you will know that I am in my Father, you are in me, and I am in you."* The Holy Spirit mediates the fullness of God the Trinity to us, and his indwelling presence empowers us to love God and do his will. Jesus sums up this intimate empowering relationship: *"If anyone loves me, he will keep my word. My Father will love him, and we will come to him and make our home with him."*

Do you know the great love God has for you? Have you received his Spirit who pours that love into your heart? How can you allow God's loving presence empower you to do his will?

REFLECT AND RESPOND

What is Jesus saying to me right now?

What step of faith is Jesus calling me to take today?

DAY 51

READ AND LISTEN: JOHN 14:27-31

Take a minute to listen for what God is saying in these verses…

COMMENT AND CONSIDER

Jesus and his closest disciples were still in that upper room where Jesus had reinterpreted the Passover supper in light of his impending death on a cross. For some time now, they had been reclining around the table listening to Jesus' teaching and responding to his questions. As their time around the table came to an end and Jesus prepared to lead them out of the walled city and up to the Garden of Gethsemane, he turned once again to their troubled hearts.

The disciples' heads must have been spinning with all Jesus was saying to them. First, he told them he was going away to prepare a place for them. Then he told them he was coming back to take them with him. In between he said he would send the Spirit and make his home inside of them. They were confused and upset, afraid this incredible adventure was coming to an end, wondering if they were going to lose this amazing new family they had become. Just as Jesus spoke *"Peace! Be still!"* over the stormy Sea of Galilee (Mark 4:39), now he spoke peace over the storm that was building in their hearts and minds.

The Roman Empire had conquered most of the Mediterranean world, including Palestine, and promised peace to its subjugated people. The famous *Pax Romana* was based on the idea that Rome had conquered her enemies and there was no more need for war because now Caesar, the son of god, was in charge. This kind of external peace, an absence of conflict imposed at sword-point, was a hollow counterfeit compared to the true inner peace that rules the heart and mind of the person who is secure and fulfilled.

Shalom is the Hebrew word for "peace," and it stands in stark contrast to *Pax Romana*. *Shalom* is the deep wholeness of body, mind, heart, and soul that comes from living in right relationship with God, others, and the world around us. *Shalom* is to be completely satisfied and secure in God's love. *Shalom* is the standard greeting and farewell for the people of Israel. (See Exodus 4:18.) *Shalom* is integral to God's promise to his people. (See Leviticus 26:6.) *Shalom* is at the heart of God's blessing offered through Aaron and his sons. (See Numbers 6:24-26.) *Shalom* is the Psalmist's cry to God. (See Psalm 4:8.) The Prophets foretold the Messiah would come as the Prince of *Shalom*. (See Isaiah 9:6.)

When Jesus said to the disciples, *"Peace I leave with you. My peace I give to you,"* he drew from this deep biblical well of *shalom*. He was clear that the peace he offers is not simply the absence of conflict that Rome offered. This was a much deeper, more powerful sense of well-being that flows from the knowledge that God is good, that he is with us, that he is for us, and that he is greater than any power which stands against us. Even though he was going away physically, Jesus was not abandoning them. In fact, he pointed out, it would be even better for them because he will be with them through the Holy Spirit living inside of them. They will carry the authority and power to overcome the *"ruler of the world,"* their adversary, the devil himself.

Jesus was about to step into the most difficult chapter of his life on earth. He knew beatings, imprisonment, torture, and death awaited him. And yet he was able to stand in perfect peace by trusting the Father and yielding to the Spirit inside of him. He called his disciples to follow his example. Although they too would face unknown challenges and sacrifice, they didn't have to live in fear or dread. As they put their trust in Jesus and followed where he led them by his Spirit, they could also learn how to live in steadfast peace.

What challenges trouble your soul? Are you living in fear or walking by faith? Can you hear Jesus speaking *shalom* into your heart and mind? What does it mean for you to trust the Prince of Peace today?

REFLECT AND RESPOND

What is Jesus saying to me right now?

What step of faith is Jesus calling me to take today?

DAY 52

READ AND LISTEN: JOHN 15:1-8

Take a minute to listen for what God is saying in these verses…

COMMENT AND CONSIDER

Jesus lived the most fruitful life in the history of the world. Although he was a blue-collar worker, owned almost no possessions, and had no official title or position, he impacted the world for good more than any other human being. Everywhere he went people's lives improved: the hungry were fed, the outcast were welcomed, the broken were healed, and the oppressed were delivered. His short life on earth inspired a movement of love, devotion, and service that continues to ripple across the people of the world, touching hearts and changing lives for the better. How did Jesus bear such good fruit that has multiplied over 2,000 years?

As we read the Gospels, we notice an intentional rhythm to Jesus' life. Each morning he withdrew to be alone with the Father in prayer and reflection. Then he stepped into a day of fruitful mission. Every week he set aside 24 hours to rest with the people closest to him and worship with his community. Then he stepped into a week of fruitful mission. After a busy season of hard work, he led his disciples away to a desolate place for a time of rest and restoration. Then they moved into another season of fruitful mission. Occasionally, Jesus took his disciples out of the area on a longer retreat to a place where no one recognized them. Then they returned to their mission field and resumed their work.

On this last night before he was arrested, Jesus wanted to make sure his followers were crystal clear on why this intentional rhythm is so important. By this time, they had left the upper room and headed down into the Kidron Valley under a full moon on their way up to Gethsemane. As they went along, Jesus gave them a beautiful picture of fruitfulness. They were probably passing by vineyards and perhaps even people sitting around a fire burning dead branches.

Jesus said, *"I am the vine; you are the branches. The one who remains in me and I in him produces much fruit, because you can do nothing without me."* The Greek word translated *"remain"* is *meno,* which can also be translated "abide," "dwell," "stay," or "lodge." To abide is to be with someone and stay connected to them. Just as the branches stay connected to the grizzled old trunk of the grapevine in order to bear grapes, Jesus said we are to live with him and stay connected to him if we hope to live fruitful lives. The branches of a grapevine are so flimsy they need to be supported by a trellis, but the main trunk of the vine is strong and deeply rooted in the soil. This trunk of the vine is what provides all the nutrients the branches need to be fruitful.

If the branches stay connected to the trunk, they will naturally bear good fruit. If the branches fail to draw nutrients from the trunk, they will wither and die. These fruitless branches are broken off and thrown into the fire. The branches that remain in the trunk bear fruit, but every year they get pruned back so they will grow again to bear more and better fruit. The gardener does the pruning because he is the one who knows which parts of the branch are no longer needed and which parts need to be preserved. What a beautiful and vivid picture Jesus has given us, demonstrating the secret of his incredibly fruitful life!

Those who follow Jesus pattern their lives after his. Jesus modeled an intentional rhythm of daily, weekly, seasonal, and occasional abiding in order to bear more and better fruit that lasts. What is the pattern of your life? Do you abide with Jesus every day? Do you set aside 24 hours every week for rest and reconnecting? Do you schedule times of rest before and after busy seasons? Do you intentionally plan to get away occasionally for a longer time of rest and recreation? Jesus is inviting you to abide in him to bear more and better fruit.

REFLECT AND RESPOND

What is Jesus saying to me right now?

What step of faith is Jesus calling me to take today?

DAY 53

READ AND LISTEN: JOHN 15:9-17

Take a minute to listen for what God is saying in these verses…

COMMENT AND CONSIDER

Throughout the ages people have been driven by the pursuit of happiness. And yet, despite all the personal wealth, scientific advancement, and technological innovation of the modern world, people today are not any more satisfied or fulfilled than they were in the time of Jesus. What is the secret of joy and a life of fulfillment? Jesus tells us it is the same as the secret of fruitfulness: abiding in him.

To abide in Jesus is to abide in his love. Jesus is God and God is love, so to abide in Jesus is to abide in love. (See 1 John 4:8.) The Greek word for love here is *agapeo*. This is the self-giving kind of love that always seeks the best for the other. Jesus wants the best for you, and he has the power to give you what is best. To abide in Jesus is to be immersed in his perfect, unconditional, unstoppable love that affirms your worth and always seeks the best for you. This is the secret of true and lasting joy.

Jesus points out that when we choose our own will over God's will, we cut ourselves off from his love. Conversely, when we submit to God's will and walk in his ways, we open ourselves up to his love. It is not that Jesus withholds his love from us; it is that we remove ourselves from him when we disobey. Jesus submitted to the Father and always did what he saw the Father doing. (See John 5:19.) Jesus listened to the Father and simply spoke the words the Father gave him to speak. (See John 12:49-50.) We are called to the same life of intimate abiding by submitting, listening, receiving, and responding in faith. This is what it means to abide in Jesus' love.

"I have told you these things so that my joy may be in you and your joy may be complete." To abide in Jesus' love is to know complete joy. This is not only the joy of receiving his love, but also the joy of allowing that love to overflow from

our lives into the lives of others. *"This is my command: Love one another as I have loved you."* The fruit borne in the lives of those who learn to abide in Jesus is an unconditional, self-giving love for those around us. The test of true love is the willingness to give up what we want for the benefit of others. *"No one has greater love than this: to lay down his life for his friends."* Jesus loved us in this way, and his love empowers us to follow his example. Here is our greatest joy, giving ourselves for the sake of others. This is what Jesus meant when he said, *"It is more blessed to give than to receive."* (Acts 20:35)

As their rabbi, Jesus was a spiritual parent to his disciples for three intensive years. But now they had reached the maturity of adult children. This is when you move from a parent-child relationship to a peer relationship: *"I do not call you servants anymore, because a servant doesn't know what his master is doing. I have called you friends, because I have made known to you everything I have heard from my Father."* The disciples had grown up, and now they were ready to make disciples of their own and become spiritual parents to others.

"I appointed you to go and produce fruit and that your fruit should remain..." As spiritual children we are meant to grow up and become spiritual parents who have spiritual children and grandchildren and great-grandchildren of our own! This is the fruit we are meant to bear. Fruit that bears the seeds of reproduction is fruit that remains. When our disciples are making disciples and our spiritual children are raising children of their own, then our fruit will remain. This is the secret of complete joy. Are you learning to abide in Jesus' love so that love can overflow into the lives of others? Are you growing up in Christ so that you can become a spiritual parent to others, and they can do the same?

REFLECT AND RESPOND

What is Jesus saying to me right now?

What step of faith is Jesus calling me to take today?

DAY 54

READ AND LISTEN: JOHN 15:18-25

Take a minute to listen for what God is saying in these verses…

COMMENT AND CONSIDER

Jesus had just finished calling the disciples to abide in his great love, but then he turned to address the world's hatred for them. Jesus only ever did good, but from the very beginning of his life on earth, those in power sought to destroy him. Everywhere he went the forces of darkness tried to overpower him. He warned his disciples that, although they would find complete joy by abiding in his love and sharing that love with each other, they would also have to face a dark and hostile world that would seek to destroy them as it sought to destroy him. *"If the world hates you, understand that it hated me before it hated you."*

John records the incredible promise that *"God loved the world in this way: He gave his one and only Son, so that everyone who believes in him will not perish but have eternal life."* (John 3:16) The Greek word translated *"world"* here is *kosmos,* which refers to the sum total of all people on Earth. God loves the whole *kosmos.* Jesus came for everyone and didn't condemn or reject anyone, but he didn't ignore the darkness and evil of the world either. He confronted those who hypocritically used power to oppress others. He did battle with the forces of evil that enslaved people. In the end he laid down his life in the ultimate act of self-giving love to break the power of sin and darkness and redeem the whole world.

That cosmic redemption of all things has begun but is still to be completed. When Jesus returns on clouds of glory, he will once and for all destroy sin, death, evil, and the devil. But until then those who follow Jesus have to confront the darkness of this not-yet-fully-redeemed world. Jesus said if we conform to the twisted values and norms of a broken world, we will not face these conflicts. It is because we follow a different King and live according to the values and norms of a different Kingdom that we have to deal with the hatred of the kingdoms of this world. *"If you were of the world, the world would love you as its own. However, because you are not of the world, but I have chosen you out of it, the world hates you."* The degree to which we follow the example of Jesus and live according to the values of his Kingdom is the degree to which we will face rejection and persecution as he did.

Jesus tells us the reason for this persecution is that they don't know God. *"But they will do all these things to you on account of my name, because they don't know the one who sent me."* However, he also says those who are aware of Jesus' teaching and miracles but still oppose his followers are accountable, because they had the opportunity to know the truth but rejected it. *"If I had not done the works among them that no one else has done, they would not be guilty of sin. Now they have seen and hated both me and my Father."*

So how should we, as followers of Jesus, relate to the world around us? Some withdraw from the world, rejecting it completely, insulating themselves from its corrupting influence. Others embrace the world, naively unaware of its power to twist the truth and lead them astray. Jesus charted a different course for us. He entered the world, confident that his light scatters the darkness and the darkness cannot overcome it. (See John 1:5.) He calls us to be *"the salt of the earth"* and *"the light of the world."* (Matthew 5:13-14) Later that evening he gave his disciples the powerful promise, *"You will have suffering in this world. Be courageous! I have conquered the world."* (John 16:33)

Are you prepared to face the challenges of following Jesus in a broken and fallen world? Do you err on the side of being too naive or too afraid of the darkness in this world? How will you love the world as God does while not being overcome by it?

REFLECT AND RESPOND

What is Jesus saying to me right now?

What step of faith is Jesus calling me to take today?

FOOTSTEPS EVERY WEEK: REVIEW

Write a brief summary of what Jesus said to you each day this past week and the step of faith he called you to take:

MONDAY

TUESDAY

WEDNESDAY

THURSDAY

FRIDAY

SATURDAY

FOOTSTEPS EVERY WEEK: REFLECT

BIG PICTURE

As you look over what Jesus has said to you this past week, do you see any themes? What is the most important thing you need to remember and believe?

PREDICTABLE PATTERN

As you look over what Jesus called you to do this past week, is there a new predictable pattern he is inviting you to establish in your life with God and others?

PLANT THE WORD

As you look over the readings from this past week, write out the passage that feels most important for you and memorize it over the next week:

DAY 55

READ AND LISTEN: JOHN 15:26-16:7

Take a minute to listen for what God is saying in these verses…

COMMENT AND CONSIDER

Jesus promised the troubled disciples he would send them the *"Counselor… the Spirit of truth who proceeds from the Father."* He explained why they would be better off when he left them: *"It is for your benefit that I go away, because if I don't go away the Counselor will not come to you. If I go, I will send him to you."* We saw earlier that this Greek word *paracletos* can be translated "Counselor," "Advocate," "Comforter," "Intercessor," or "Helper." Counselor and Advocate evoke the image of a trial lawyer who represents us, speaks for us, and defends us in court. This meaning was especially poignant to the early followers of Jesus who faced increasing levels of persecution and were put on trial for their faith.

Jesus was preparing them for the rigors of persecution that lay ahead. Not only was he going to be accused, condemned, tortured, and executed, but eventually many of his followers would face this fate as well. In Galilee he had told them, *"You are blessed when they insult you and persecute you and falsely say every kind of evil against you because of me. Be glad and rejoice, because your reward is great in heaven. For that is how they persecuted the prophets who were before you."* (Matthew 5:11-12) By prophesying the preemptive warning that this persecution was coming, Jesus gave them time to prepare so they would not be caught off guard or surprised. (See also Mark 13:9-10.)

In addition to persecution, he prophesied the coming of the Holy Spirit who would fill them, guide them, and give them the courage they needed to face these challenges. His promise planted the faith in their hearts they would need to press on in the face of such hostility. Jesus told them the Spirit would help them testify about him when called upon to give an account of their faith. Not only does the Spirit represent us as our Advocate, and guide us as our Counselor, he also functions as a witness who testifies about Jesus. Earlier Jesus told them, *"So when they arrest you and hand you over, don't worry beforehand what you will say, but say whatever is given to you at that time, for it isn't you speaking, but the Holy Spirit."* (Mark 13:11) The Spirit is a corroborating witness who shows us how to be a faithful witness and gives our testimony credibility.

Then Jesus got more specific in his prophecy, telling them plainly, *"They will ban you from the synagogues."* Earlier John told us this had already begun to take place when Jesus healed the blind man at the Pool of Siloam. (See John 9:22-23.) Even worse, Jesus told them, there would be those who were so zealous to protect their false religion they would kill them and believe they were serving God.

We know this is exactly what Saul the Pharisee did to the early followers of Jesus in Jerusalem. Working as an agent of the Sanhedrin, Saul supervised the illegal stoning of Stephen and organized a campaign of terror against the Christian communities in Jerusalem and Damascus, all out of his conviction he was serving God. (See Acts 8:1-3; 9:1-2.) Years later, after Saul had become Paul the Apostle of Jesus Christ, he addressed a mob of religious Jews who in turn wanted to kill him, *"I was zealous for God, just as all of you are today. I persecuted this Way to the death, arresting and putting both men and women in jail…"* (Acts 22:3-4)

When all these things started happening, the followers of Jesus remembered these prophecies that Jesus spoke and realized it was happening just as he had foretold. They also remembered his promise that the Counselor would testify for them and through them so they could be courageous witnesses to Jesus and his coming Kingdom, even at the cost of their own lives.

How do Jesus' prophetic warnings and promises affect you? Even if your life and physical well-being are not being threatened, how can you allow the Holy Spirit to give you the strength and courage you need to be an effective witness to Jesus and his Good News?

REFLECT AND RESPOND

What is Jesus saying to me right now?

What step of faith is Jesus calling me to take today?

DAY 56

READ AND LISTEN: JOHN 16:8-15

Take a minute to listen for what God is saying in these verses…

COMMENT AND CONSIDER

Jesus already told his followers the Advocate would shift from lawyer to witness and *"testify about me."* He had also promised them the Counselor would help them to be a courageous and effective witness when they were on trial. But then Jesus explained how the Advocate would ultimately turn the tables on those who prosecuted them: *"When he comes, he will convict the world about sin, righteousness, and judgment…"* Now, instead of the followers of Jesus being on trial, the world itself will be examined and judged by the Spirit himself!

Jesus said there are three aspects to this prosecution of the world: sin, righteousness, and judgment. Jesus himself had addressed all these issues during his earthly ministry. Jesus demonstrated and preached the Good News of a Kingdom where grace and love prevail. He did not come to condemn the world but to save the world. (See John 3:17.) Yet Jesus called people to confess and reject sin. (See John 5:14; 8:11.) He invited people into a new covenant where righteousness is offered as a free gift of grace. (See Matthew 3:15; 6:33.) And he warned them the end is coming when he will return to judge the devil and all those who have chosen evil over good. (See John 12:31.)

It is not our job to convict others of sin, make people righteous, or judge anyone but ourselves. This was the work of Jesus on earth, and now it is the work of the Spirit. The work of the Spirit is the continuation of the movement Jesus began. He is the one who convicts the human heart and leads us from error and deception into the freedom of the truth. There is a clear baton-pass from Jesus to the Spirit and from the Spirit to the followers of Jesus.

Jesus is indisputably the greatest Teacher of all time. And yet, in his three short years of public ministry he did not have enough time to give his followers everything they needed to fulfill their mission. Nor were they ready to receive it. *"I still have many things to tell you, but you can't bear them now.*" So he sent the Spirit to continue his teaching ministry: *"When the Spirit of truth comes, he will guide you into all the truth."* It is not just that the Spirit continues the mission of Jesus, but the Spirit also fills Jesus' followers and empowers them to continue doing what Jesus did!

On the day of Pentecost, the Holy Spirit was poured out on the believers, and they began to proclaim the Good News of the Kingdom in ways they never could have without the Spirit's empowerment. When Peter, an ordinary fisherman, proclaimed the message of Jesus, three thousand people came to faith and were baptized. (See Acts 2:14-41.) Not long after this, Peter and John healed the lame man at the Beautiful Gate in the inner Temple Courts, and five thousand came to faith. (See Acts 3:1-4:4.) When the religious leaders of Jerusalem *"realized that they were uneducated and untrained men, they were amazed and recognized that they had been with Jesus."* (Acts 4:13)

The Spirit of Truth continued the work Jesus began by empowering ordinary men and women to proclaim the Good News and do what Jesus did! The rest of the New Testament is the written record of how the Spirit inspired ordinary people to continue what Jesus had begun. (See 2 Peter 1:20-21.) Still today the Spirit of Truth guides us into the truth as we read Scripture and plants faith in our hearts to respond to his Word. Still today the Spirit of Truth activates the gift of prophecy and gives us pictures, words, dreams, and visions that are meant to help others and build up the Body of Christ. (See 1 Corinthians 14:1, 26-33.)

Are you open to the conviction of the Holy Spirit in your life? Do you ask the Spirit to guide you into all the truth? Are you learning to let the Spirit empower you to continue the mission Jesus began by speaking that truth and doing the things Jesus did?

REFLECT AND RESPOND

What is Jesus saying to me right now?

What step of faith is Jesus calling me to take today?

DAY 57

READ AND LISTEN: JOHN 16:16-33

Take a minute to listen for what God is saying in these verses…

COMMENT AND CONSIDER

I often wish I was one of Jesus' first disciples, walking through the streets of Jerusalem with him, but then I realize how confusing it must have been. Jesus told them, *"In a little while, you will no longer see me; again in a little while, you will see me."* The disciples whispered among themselves, trying to make sense of all the comings and goings. They admitted, *"We don't know what he's talking about."* Sensing their confusion, Jesus used more metaphors to prepare them for the tumult that was soon to engulf them.

Jesus told them it was like a war where one people mourn over the battles lost, while the victors rejoice. But then the outcome suddenly flip-flops, the conquered become the conquerors, and those grieving begin to rejoice. Jesus told them it was like a woman caught up in the travail of labor, racked with pain and unsure of the outcome. But when the child has been safely delivered, the mother is so filled with joy that she can't even remember the labor pains.

Jesus was still speaking to them in *"figures of speech."* He had done this throughout his ministry, teaching them in parables, similes, and word-pictures. *"The kingdom of God is like…"* *"A man had two sons…"* *"Unless you become like this little child…"* *"Take the log out of your own eye…"* When the disciples asked him why he spoke this way, Jesus' answer was even more confusing. Quoting Isaiah 6:9-10 he said, *"I speak to them in parables, because looking they do not see, and hearing they do not listen or understand."* (Matthew 13:13)

Was Jesus using figures of speech so people had to wrestle with his meaning and come to a deeper understanding? Was he giving them these stories and word pictures so people wouldn't take his words and twist them into something he never intended? Or were the parables and pictures simply meant to help them remember and pass on these truths to others? It is still hard for us to understand everything Jesus said and did because we have to overcome our many preconceptions.

The disciples were so shaped by their preconceptions of what the Messiah would do, they couldn't understand the dramatic events which were about to unfold. In hindsight we can see Jesus was talking about his impending execution followed by his glorious resurrection. But perhaps Jesus was also talking about the bigger picture, that we who live now benefit from the light of his first coming, but still live in anticipation of the final redemption of all things at his return. In this way we are like those first disciples, still waiting and wondering exactly how it is all going to unfold.

Jesus told the disciples that one day it would all become clear. *"A time is coming when I will no longer speak to you in figures, but I will tell you plainly about the Father."* Was he referring to the teaching he would give them during the forty days between his resurrection and ascension? Or did he mean the Spirit would inspire Apostles like Paul to give clearer explanations? Or was he referring to the clarity that will come when he returns, tears down every obstacle to the truth, and removes the scales from our eyes so we see all things clearly?

The disciples thought they had already gotten clarity: *"Look, now you're speaking plainly and not using any figurative language."* But Jesus warned them not to be overconfident: *"Do you now believe? Indeed, an hour is coming, and has come, when each of you will be scattered to his own home, and you will leave me alone."* All of us live in the in-between time when we *"see only a reflection as in a mirror."* (1 Corinthians 13:12) There are clear and certain truths on which we can confidently build our lives, but until Jesus returns, there will still be unresolved mysteries.

How do you interpret Jesus' figures of speech? What things are clear and what things are yet to be revealed? How do you trust Jesus and follow him even though you don't have all the answers?

REFLECT AND RESPOND

What is Jesus saying to me right now?

What step of faith is Jesus calling me to take today?

DAY 58

READ AND LISTEN: JOHN 17:1-19

Take a minute to listen for what God is saying in these verses…

COMMENT AND CONSIDER

While he taught them, Jesus and the disciples had been making their way out of the walled city of Jerusalem, through the Kidron Valley, and up to the Garden of Gethsemane at the foot of the Mount of Olives. Perhaps it was when they arrived at that place on the Mount of Olives that Jesus stopped and prayed this prayer for the disciples. It is the longest recorded prayer of Jesus in the Bible, and the last time Jesus would pray over his followers before his arrest. He knew his final hour was drawing near, so he turned to his Father in prayer for the strength he and his disciples needed to finish their mission.

His prayer began with an affirmation of his identity. *"Father, the hour has come. Glorify your Son so that the Son may glorify you."* Everything Jesus said and did flowed from his relationship with the Father. His identity, as declared at his baptism and transfiguration, came from the Father: *"This is my beloved Son, with whom I am well-pleased."* (Matthew 3:17; 17:5) From this identity Jesus drew his authority. Because his Father is the King of the Universe, Jesus knew he was an authorized representative of the King by virtue of his identity as the Son. This is how the power of the Spirit flowed through Jesus to do the will of his Father.

Jesus' mission was to bring abundant, eternal life to everyone who would receive him and become a child of God. (See John 1:4-5, 12-13.) Now, as Jesus prayed for his followers, he clearly defined this new life they received: *"This is eternal life: that they may know you, the only true God, and the one you have sent—Jesus Christ."* This knowing is not just the intellectual understanding of ideas or doctrines, but an intimate relational knowing between persons. At the end, those who know God will sit at the King's table for the great feast of the Messiah, but those who don't will knock on the door, and the Master will say, *"I don't know you or where you're from."* (Luke 13:25)

"

Through their relationship, Jesus brought the disciples into a relationship with God. He prayed, *"I have revealed your name to the people you gave me from the world."* Since Jesus simply did what he saw the Father doing and spoke the words the Father gave him to speak (see John 5:19; 12:49-50), the disciples knew what they received from Jesus was coming from the Father. This is what gave them confidence to follow the example of Jesus and trust his teaching. *"Now they know that everything you have given me is from you, because I have given them the words you gave me."*

Since Jesus knew he would soon be gone physically, he prayed for the Father to protect and guide the disciples as they carried out their mission to bring Good News to the ends of the earth. *"They are not of the world, just as I am not of the world... As you sent me into the world, I also have sent them into the world."* As a preexistent member of the Trinity, Jesus left his place of eternal glory and power at the right hand of the Father, emptied himself, and entered this broken and fallen world. He loved the world but refused to be shaped or defined by the world. He showed the disciples how to walk this path of being in the world, but not of the world.

Unlike the religious leaders of his time, Jesus did not separate himself from those considered "sinners" but entered their broken lives with redeeming love. However, he never compromised the truth or succumbed to the influence of sin and evil.

He was the light of the world and the salt of the earth, and he called his disciples to be the same. (See Matthew 5:13-16.) How is Jesus calling you to be *in the world* for the sake of the lost? What are the ways you can keep from being *of the world* by influencing others rather than being influenced by the world?

REFLECT AND RESPOND

What is Jesus saying to me right now?

What step of faith is Jesus calling me to take today?

DAY 59

READ AND LISTEN: JOHN 17:20-26

Take a minute to listen for what God is saying in these verses…

COMMENT AND CONSIDER

In the biblical world, relationships were defined by covenants. When a family established a farm, they made covenants with their neighbors. They promised not to steal their neighbor's livestock or crops and to help protect that family if bandits attacked. Their neighbors made the same promises in return, believing these promises that bound them together in a relationship of mutual trust. Kings made covenants with the rulers of neighboring states in a similar way. In our culture we are still familiar with the covenant of marriage, when two people make vows of love and fidelity, and their mutual trust in these sacred promises binds them together as one.

The personal relationship with God that Jesus made possible for us is based on the New Covenant of grace, which he inaugurated in his baptism and ratified by his blood shed on the cross. It began when Jesus invited people to follow him. Discipleship shapes our covenantal relationship with God through Jesus. As disciples we are bound to our rabbi who raises us up to know what he knows and do what he does. Disciples are meant to become rabbis who invite disciples into the same kind of covenant relationship. Those covenantal relationships multiply when we invite others to follow us as we follow Jesus. (See 1 Corinthians 11:1.)

Jesus prayed for our covenantal oneness: *"May they all be one, as you, Father, are in me and I am in you."* Jesus' relationship with the Father makes our relationship with God possible, but it is also a model of how we are to relate to one another. Earlier that night Jesus had given them a new commandment, *"Love one another. Just as I have loved you"* (John 13:34) Jesus prayed that we would live in the same kind of loving oneness with each other as we see Jesus living with his heavenly Father.

This language raises an important question about the Person of Jesus: is the oneness of Jesus with the Father the same as our oneness with Jesus and the Father? The answer is yes and no. Yes, because in his humanity Jesus modeled the kind of relationship with the Father we are to have with the Father, Son, and Holy Spirit. No, because Jesus is the pre-existent second person of the Trinity who emptied himself and took on our full humanity for thirty-some years while he walked on this earth. He did not forfeit his full divinity when he became fully human, but he chose to live out of his humanity in order to give us an example to follow.

So, although Jesus is God and has a unique ontological oneness with the Father as a member of the Trinity, by faith he also models for us a relationship of covenantal oneness with the Father. That means we are to imitate the way Jesus related to his heavenly Father during his life on earth. It also means we are to imitate his relationship with the disciples in our relationships with each other. Jesus established a spiritual family in which he operated as a spiritual Father and taught the disciples to live as brothers and sisters. This is the way we are called to relate to each other as well.

The Holy Spirit is the spiritual glue who binds all these relationships together, because he mediates the presence of the Father and the Son to those who believe in Jesus. *"I am in them and you are in me, so that they may be made completely one, that the world may know you have sent me and have loved them as you have loved me."* The presence of the Holy Spirit within the heart and life of every believer makes it possible for the Father and the Son to make their home inside of us. This is how we show his love to the world. (See John 14:23.)

What is keeping you from living in covenantal oneness with the other believers around you? How can you learn from Jesus' example to live in a closer relationship with God and others?

Reflect and Respond

What is Jesus saying to me right now?

What step of faith is Jesus calling me to take today?

DAY 60

READ AND LISTEN: JOHN 18:1-11

Take a minute to listen for what God is saying in these verses…

COMMENT AND CONSIDER

At the base of the Mount of Olives, across the Kidron Valley from the Temple Mount, stands a grove of ancient olive trees. They don't date to the time of Jesus, because the Roman army cut down every tree on the Mount of Olives when they laid siege to Jerusalem in AD 70, but the trees are well over 1,600 years old. This area was known as the Garden of Gethsemane, meaning "the place of olive pressing." A modern church there, built on the foundation of ancient churches, marks the place where Jesus went to pray that final Passover night.

Archaeologists have discovered a first-century olive oil press in a nearby cave, which may have been the place where Jesus and the disciples slept on the Mount of Olives when it was too late to go all the way back to Bethany. (See Luke 21:37.) This would explain why Judas knew to bring the soldiers there to arrest Jesus. The Synoptic Gospels tell us Jesus went into the grove to pour out his heart to the Father. After three gut-wrenching prayers, he was ready to face the terrible fate that awaited him at Golgotha.

Judas left during the Passover meal to alert the religious authorities to Jesus' whereabouts so they could arrest him under cover of darkness and avoid provoking a reaction from the crowds. Judas would have taken them first to the house of the upper room, where he left Jesus. Discovering them already gone, he took them to the next most likely spot, the place where they sometimes spent the night. Judas arrived with *"a company of soldiers and some officials,"* which would have been made up of the Temple Police who answered to the Sanhedrin and possibly some Roman soldiers who had been seconded to the High Priest.

When Judas and the soldiers arrived, Jesus was not surprised. Prophetically he knew what was coming, so he went out to meet them. When they asked for Jesus of Nazareth, he said, *"I am he"* and the power of his words knocked over

Judas and the soldiers. This is another instance where Jesus identified himself using the name of God, *"I am,"* as a sign of his divinity. John makes it crystal clear that Jesus willingly submitted to his arrest. He could have easily slipped over the Mount of Olives before they arrived and disappeared eastward into the nearby desert wilderness where he had spent 40 days fasting.

Peter did not understand Jesus was submitting willingly to this arrest, so he reacted as a good covenant partner should in the face of danger by swinging his sword at Malchus, the servant of the High Priest, cutting off his ear. Jesus rebuked Peter, *"Put your sword away! Am I not to drink the cup the Father has given me?"* Luke, the physician, records that Jesus healed Malchus' ear, quite a contrast to the brutality that would soon be shown to Jesus. Any time a minor character in the story is named in the Gospels, it is a hint that person was present in the community to whom the Apostles were preaching and writing. Malchus most likely became a follower of Jesus and lived to tell his story to the early Christian community.

Although he taught his followers to turn the other cheek, Jesus was not against self-protection. In fact, earlier that evening he told the disciples trouble was coming and they should make sure they had a couple of swords to protect themselves. (See Luke 22:35-38.) But in this case, Jesus knew he was to submit even though the charges against him were false and those prosecuting them were corrupt. He told his disciples, *"Or do you think that I cannot call on my Father, and he will provide me here and now with more than twelve legions of angels? How, then, would the Scriptures be fulfilled that say it must happen this way?"* (Matthew 26:53-54) The point was Jesus chose to submit because he knew it was his destiny.

How do you know when to fight evil and when to submit? What does it mean to you that Jesus went to the cross willingly?

REFLECT AND RESPOND

What is Jesus saying to me right now?

What step of faith is Jesus calling me to take today?

FOOTSTEPS EVERY WEEK: REVIEW

Write a brief summary of what Jesus said to you each day this past week and the step of faith he called you to take:

MONDAY

TUESDAY

WEDNESDAY

THURSDAY

FRIDAY

SATURDAY

FOOTSTEPS EVERY WEEK: REFLECT

BIG PICTURE

As you look over what Jesus has said to you this past week, do you see any themes? What is the most important thing you need to remember and believe?

PREDICTABLE PATTERN

As you look over what Jesus called you to do this past week, is there a new predictable pattern he is inviting you to establish in your life with God and others?

PLANT THE WORD

As you look over the readings from this past week, write out the passage that feels most important for you and memorize it over the next week:

DAY 61

READ AND LISTEN: JOHN 18:12-27

Take a minute to listen for what God is saying in these verses…

COMMENT AND CONSIDER

At Mount Sinai God appointed Moses' older brother Aaron as leader of the priests serving in the Tabernacle, decreeing the office would pass down to his sons. (See Exodus 28:1; Leviticus 8:1-9.) His tribe, the tribe of Levi, became the priests who took on the various functions of the sacrificial system. After the time of King David and King Solomon, the High Priest was chosen from the descendants of Zadok, the leading priest during their time. Following the Babylonian exile and the rebuilding of the Temple, the Levitical priests served as musicians, guards, and janitors in the Temple courts, while the descendants of Zadok became the priests who carried out the sacrifices in the Temple itself. The High Priests were chosen by the king from the aristocratic priestly families of Jerusalem.

When Herod the Great began to rule on behalf of the Romans in 37 BC, he and his sons appointed and deposed High Priests from the aristocratic families of Jerusalem based on their willingness to serve the purposes of Rome rather than their lineage. In AD 6, when the Romans began to rule Judea and Jerusalem directly, their governors chose the High Priests and dismissed them at will. The first of these High Priests appointed by the Roman governor Quirinius was Ananus ben Seth, also known as Annas. He served for ten years before being deposed in AD 15. However, Annas retained tremendous power over the next 20 years through his five sons who eventually served as High Priest, in addition to his son-in-law Caiaphas.

Properly known as Joseph ben Caiaphas, he was appointed High Priest in AD 18 and ruled until AD 36, some 19 years, the longest tenure of the first century. Most of the High Priests in that period only ruled for a year or two, which tells us Caiaphas was unusually skilled at political diplomacy. In 1990 construction workers stumbled upon a first-century family tomb containing 12 limestone bone boxes called ossuaries. One of these was elaborately decorated and inscribed with the name "Joseph ben Caiaphas." This sensational discovery points to the historical accuracy of the Gospel accounts and the importance of this high priestly family.

John tells us Jesus was bound and brought first to the house of Annas to be examined by the former High Priest. The office of High Priest was originally meant to be for life, which may reflect why Annas had so much influence despite the fact he no longer held an official title. After asking him some questions, Annas sent Jesus to Caiaphas and a select group of the Sanhedrin, the Jewish ruling council over which he presided, who began the formal proceedings against Jesus.

Peter and *"another disciple"* (probably John) followed Jesus right into the courtyard of the High Priests house, drawing on John's connections with the High Priest. Despite abandoning Jesus and fleeing when he was arrested, this was an incredible act of courage! In the glow of the courtyard fire where Peter warmed himself, the servants began identifying him as a follower of Jesus, but Peter denied it. The third one to recognize Peter was a relative of Malchus, whose ear Peter had cut off earlier that night. When Peter denied knowing Jesus the third time, he heard the rooster crow, a painful reminder that Jesus had prophesied this very moment of catastrophic failure.

Peter was afraid for his life, knowing his rabbi was on trial before those who wanted him dead. And yet how often do we fail to speak up, change the conversation, or otherwise downplay our relationship with Jesus simply because we are embarrassed, not wanting to offend and afraid others will think less of us? Can you hear the rooster crowing? Will you allow that conviction to give you greater courage? How will you take more opportunities to talk with others about your relationship with Jesus?

REFLECT AND RESPOND

What is Jesus saying to me right now?

What step of faith is Jesus calling me to take today?

DAY 62

READ AND LISTEN: JOHN 18:28-40

Take a minute to listen for what God is saying in these verses…

COMMENT AND CONSIDER

Herod the Great built an enormous palace complex on the western hill of Jerusalem, second only to the Temple courts in size and splendor. It was comprised of two large courtyard buildings, one on either end of a vast paved pavilion, surrounded by a strong defensive wall. The ends of the two buildings which faced one another featured a raised platform, called the *bema*, where the ruler could make public pronouncements, adjudicate criminal and civil cases, and address large crowds which gathered in the plaza. John uses the Aramaic term *gabbatha*, meaning "stone pavement," to describe this complex. (John 19:13)

The western wall of the palace was incorporated into what are still the city walls, and the northern end was fortified with three huge defensive towers. The base of the largest tower stands just inside the modern Jaffa Gate today, and is erroneously called the "Tower of David." This tower base is now part of the Citadel, a Crusader castle built out of the ruins of Herod's Palace, surrounded by a dry moat and featuring classic elements of a medieval European fortress. It was from here that the Crusader kings of Jerusalem ruled during the eleventh century AD.

Upon his death, Herod the Great's massive palace became the residence of his son Archelaus for ten years. Once Archelaus was deposed in AD 6, the palace became the official residence of the Roman governors when they visited the Holy City for special occasions. And so, after the Sanhedrin convicted Jesus of the capital offense of blasphemy, they brought him from Caiaphas' house on the southwest hill to *the governor's headquarters*, meaning the nearby palace of Herod, to seek an audience with Pilate, the Roman governor who was visiting Jerusalem for the Passover festival.

It was early morning on that Friday, which is the time when Roman officials made themselves available to hear grievances and pass judgment on disputes.

When John says the Jewish religious leaders could not enter the palace buildings for fear of defilement and specifies *"Pilate came out to them,"* it indicates the governor stood on one of the judgment platforms addressing them as they gathered a crowd of supporters in the plaza. The religious leaders could not bring the charge of blasphemy to Pilate because he would simply dismiss the case as a matter of Jewish religion, so instead they accused Jesus of claiming to be king in place of Caesar. (See John 19:12.)

Sensing the manipulation of the religious leaders, Pilate took Jesus inside the palace itself so he could cross-examine him privately. He asked Jesus, *"Are you the king of the Jews?"* Jesus answered affirmatively when he explained, *"My kingdom is not of this world."* Pilate persisted in asking about his royal identity, and Jesus responded by testifying his Kingship is a revelation of truth in contrast to the lies of those seeking to destroy him. Almost in despair, the governor asked the searching question, *"What is truth?"* Pilate was savvy enough as a politician to know when he was being lied to and when he was being told the truth.

This exchange convinced Pilate Jesus was not guilty of any capital offense, and he perceived that the religious leaders were trying to deceive him. So he appealed to the crowd based on the practice of offering amnesty to a popular figure for the Passover holiday. When Pilate offered to set Jesus free, the religious leaders stirred up the crowd to demand the release of a rebel murderer named Barabbas instead. (See Matthew 27:20.) The bitter irony is that Barabbas was, in fact, guilty of the very crime the religious leaders were trying to pin on Jesus: insurrection. Jesus literally took Barabbas' place by taking on the guilt and punishment that Barabbas deserved, which is exactly what he would do for the whole world by dying on the cross!

How have you wrestled with the truth of Jesus' identity and role in your life? What does it mean for you that Jesus, though innocent, took your place and endured the punishment you deserved?

REFLECT AND RESPOND

What is Jesus saying to me right now?

What step of faith is Jesus calling me to take today?

DAY 63

Read and Listen: John 19:1-16

Take a minute to listen for what God is saying in these verses…

Comment and Consider

Flogging was a terrible form of Roman punishment in which the victim was stripped naked, tied to a post, and beaten with a *flagellum*. This brutal whip consisted of a short handle bound to multiple strips of leather embedded with sharp pieces of metal or bone that literally tore the flesh from the victim's back. The Jewish historian Josephus tells us that flogging often exposed the ribcage and internal organs and that sometimes those who received it didn't survive. Flogging could be used as a stand-alone form of punishment, but it was also the required precursor to a crucifixion.

Although convinced he was innocent, Pilate ordered Jesus to be flogged in hopes of placating the crowd which was calling for his crucifixion, but to no avail. (See Luke 23:16, 22.) Purple cloth was normally reserved for royalty and aristocrats because the dye which came from Murex sea snails—one drop per snail—was extremely expensive. Most likely the Roman soldiers mocked Jesus by wrapping him in a faded soldier's robe, called a *sagum*, which were typically scarlet. (See Matthew 27:28.) There are other reports of Roman soldiers in Jerusalem dressing up revolutionary prisoners as mock "kings" and rolling dice to determine their fate. Little did they know that as they forced the sharp thorns onto Jesus' scalp, slapped his face, and derided him as *"king of the Jews,"* he was, in fact, the greatest King to ever to walk the face of the earth.

Coming back out onto the *bema* platform to address the religious leaders and their hand-picked mob, Pilate reported the results of his cross-examination: *"Look, I'm bringing him out to you to let you know I find no grounds for charging him."* Then they led out the prisoner, beaten and bleeding underneath the mock robe and thorns, showing them the brutal punishment Jesus had already endured, famously declaring, *"Here is the man!"* The sight of Jesus, battered and torn, should have evoked compassion or at least revulsion, but the religious leaders led the crowds to demand even more, chanting *"Crucify!*

Crucify!" Pilate reiterated his judgment that Jesus was innocent, so the religious leaders revealed the real reason they condemned Jesus. It wasn't that Jesus was a military revolutionary threatening Rome; it was his claim to be the Son of God that threatened the authority and power of the religious leaders.

When Pilate heard Jesus' claim of divinity, it scared him. Roman religion viewed the gods as capricious and punitive. Much of Roman religious practice centered around placating the gods and avoiding their wrath. Pilate did not want to unknowingly anger the gods by executing one of their sons. So he brought Jesus back inside the palace and resumed his questioning. When Jesus refused to answer, Pilate reminded him he alone held the power of life and death, but Jesus reminded him the only authority Pilate wielded was given to him by God.

When Pilate again told the religious leaders he was going to release Jesus, they played their final card, saying, *"If you release this man, you are not Caesar's friend."* To be a friend of Caesar was to be loyal to the Emperor, supporting and defending his rule. To be an enemy of Caesar was the worst accusation a Roman could make, amounting to treason punishable by death. Roman officials were regularly deposed, exiled, or executed when the Emperor perceived they were no longer his friends. In fact, Tiberius Caesar accused Lucius Aelius Sejanus, Pilate's primary patron back in Rome, of conspiring to overthrow him and had Sejanus executed in AD 31, shortly before or after Jesus' crucifixion.

In the end, Pilate decided the risk to his own political position and power was too great to do what he knew was right. Instead, he knowingly condemned an innocent man to the most gruesome kind of execution: crucifixion. When was the last time you had to wrestle with a question of right and wrong? Did you do the right thing? When did you give in to the temptation to do what you knew was wrong? What risk would you take, or price would you pay to do the right thing?

REFLECT AND RESPOND

What is Jesus saying to me right now?

What step of faith is Jesus calling me to take today?

DAY 64

READ AND LISTEN: JOHN 19:17-22

Take a minute to listen for what God is saying in these verses…

COMMENT AND CONSIDER

Crucifixion was the most torturous form of execution in the Roman Empire. The Romans adapted it from the Persians, who had adapted it from the Assyrians. The Law of Moses recognized the extreme depravity of this type of death, saying, *"anyone hung on a tree is under God's curse."* (Deuteronomy 21:23. See also Galatians 3:13.) Roman citizens were exempt from crucifixion as it was employed primarily to shock and terrify subject populations into submission. For this reason, the Romans typically chose the most visible spot beside a well-traveled road to crucify those who dared defy Imperial rule. When a group of Galilean Jews revolted in 4 BC, the Romans crucified hundreds of them, lining up their crosses along the Via Maris, the main road leading into Sepphoris, a large city near Nazareth.

After a victim was sentenced to crucifixion, they were led through the streets of the city to the place of crucifixion carrying the crossbeam of their cross. Outside of the western wall of Jerusalem, along the road that led from the Gennath ("Garden") Gate to Jaffa, lie the remains of an ancient rock quarry. From this hillside builders cut large blocks of limestone to rebuild the Temple after their return from exile in Babylon in the sixth century BC. This quarry was abandoned for centuries until it was developed into a cemetery for wealthy families who wanted to be buried as near to Jerusalem as possible. The vertical walls of sheer limestone were a perfect place to build rock-cut tombs.

On the eastern side of the rock quarry was a 20-foot-tall section of limestone that stood out from the surrounding walls. It was a section of soft and fissured limestone, not suitable for building stones, so the builders simply cut around that section, leaving a highly visible rocky outcropping. The Romans chose this rock as their place for crucifixions. Since it was just outside the city walls and beside the road to Jaffa, it was a place where many people would be forced to witness the gruesome executions they performed. This highly visible rock was given the name *"Golgotha,"* Aramaic for "the place of the skull," and it was to this rock Jesus was led to be crucified.

Once they arrived at the site of crucifixion, the victim was stripped naked, their arms stretched out along the crossbeam, and wrists either tied or nailed in place. When nailed it was using long iron spikes driven between the two bones of the lower arm, just below the wrist bones, carefully avoiding any arteries. We know Jesus was nailed to his cross because Thomas said he would only believe Jesus had risen from the dead if he could put his finger in the nail holes. When Jesus appeared to Thomas a week later, he said, *"Put your finger here and look at my hands."* (John 20:27) The Greek word translated *"hand"* here means the lower arm and hand. Once the victim was tied or nailed to it through the wrists, the crossbeam was lifted up and hung on the post, to which the heel bones of the victim's feet were then nailed.

Often the Romans affixed a *titulus* to the top of the upright post of a cross, a wooden sign declaring the crime for which crucifixion was the punishment, thus increasing the execution's deterrent factor. John reports the *titulus* at the top of Jesus' cross read *Jesus of Nazareth, the King of the Jews* in Aramaic, Latin, and Greek. This upset the religious leaders because they didn't want people to believe Jesus really was the Messiah King, but when they asked the Governor to change it, he simply replied, *"What I have written, I have written."* Pilate was getting the final word, telling the world Jesus was falsely accused and innocent of any crime. Little did he know his ironic sign declared the truth that he was brutally executing the most important man who ever lived.

Sometimes the truth is right in front of us, but we don't recognize the signs. What truth about Jesus or yourself have you been missing? What can you do to read the signs more accurately?

REFLECT AND RESPOND

What is Jesus saying to me right now?

What step of faith is Jesus calling me to take today?

DAY 65

READ AND LISTEN: JOHN 19:23-27

Take a minute to listen for what God is saying in these verses…

COMMENT AND CONSIDER

Victims of crucifixion were stripped of all their clothing, and executioners typically claimed the right to plunder any possessions that might remain. The basic unit of the Roman army was called a *contubernium* in Latin and consisted of eight soldiers who shared a tent. Often, they were split into two groups of four to carry out specific tasks, as in the case of Jesus' crucifixion. These four soldiers tore Jesus' robe and cloak into four pieces of fabric so each could claim an equal share of the humble spoils.

Jesus' inner tunic was a fine linen garment woven so there were no seams on the sides. The value of the garment would be lost if they tore it into pieces, so they decided to cast lots to see who would take it. Lots could be made of knuckle bones, small stones, or pottery shards. One was marked, and whoever drew the marked one was the winner. This scene was foretold in Psalm 22:18, another confirmation God's plan was unfolding in the midst of the bloody chaos and obscene injustice engulfing Jesus.

John tells us he was at the cross along with Mary Magdalene, Jesus' mother Mary, Mary's sister Salome, and Mary the wife of Clopas. (See also Mark 15:40.) Despite the intense pain literally crushing the life out of him, Jesus remained aware of those around him. Luke tells us he pronounced forgiveness over the soldiers who were executing him and offered assurance of salvation to the rebel on the cross next to him who expressed faith. (See Luke 23:32-43.) Then Jesus turned his attention to his mother.

Due to the circumstances of his birth, Mary was in a unique position to know her son was the Messiah. She had received revelation from the angel Gabriel, the testimony of shepherds, the prophecies of Anna and Simeon, as well as exotic visitors from the east bearing expensive gifts. So it is not surprising she would expect Jesus to do something when their friends in Cana ran out of wine at their wedding reception. (See John 2:1-12.)

But when Jesus taught from Isaiah 61 in the synagogue at Nazareth his message that the Messiah had come not just for the Jews but also for the Gentiles, it was so shocking to Mary and the entire extended family that none of them stood up for Jesus when the people tried to throw him off a cliff and stone him to death. (See Luke 4:16-30.) Jesus was not fulfilling his mother's expectations of what kind of Messiah Jesus would be. This is why he left Nazareth and established his base of operations in Capernaum in the extended family home of Simon and Andrew.

As news of Jesus' revolutionary mission filtered back to Nazareth, Mary and the family members grew increasingly concerned for Jesus, surmising he must be suffering from mental illness. So they traveled to Capernaum and stood outside the crowded home of Simon and Andrew, asking for Jesus. However, Jesus told them his family was defined by those who do the will of God. (See Mark 3:20, 31-35.) This division between Jesus and his family continued, as John himself reports, *not even his brothers believed in him.* (John 7:5) But once he was hanging on the cross, his mother had come full circle.

We don't know exactly when she finally accepted her son for the revolutionary Messiah he was meant to be, but we do know she was there among Jesus' most dedicated disciples. Wanting to make it crystal clear his mother was now part of the spiritual family he had built, Jesus referred to John when he said to her, *"Woman, here is your son."* Likewise, Jesus referred to Mary when he said to John, *"Here is your mother."* From that moment on, Mary became part of the spiritual family Jesus had built, eventually followed by his brothers James and Judas, and perhaps all of his natural family.

Who is your spiritual family? Are you trying to follow Jesus and carry out his mission alone or with others? How can you live more fully as part of a family on mission?

REFLECT AND RESPOND

What is Jesus saying to me right now?

What step of faith is Jesus calling me to take today?

DAY 66

Take a minute to listen for what God is saying in these verses…

COMMENT AND CONSIDER

Death on a cross was one of the most torturous ways to die in the ancient world. Hanging from the crossbeam, the full weight of the victim's body pulled against the spikes driven through his wrists and heel bones. As the victim hung on the cross, the muscles around the ribcage were stretched tight, constricting the expansion of the lungs. Lungs are designed to continuously pump out body fluids that naturally accumulate, but the lungs of a crucified man could not expel the fluids. As a result, their lung capacity steadily diminished as they began to slowly drown in their own fluids.

Despite the agonizing pain it produced, the human will to live is so strong that the victim of crucifixion would pull their body up with their arms and push up with their legs to relieve the pressure on the lungs, allowing a short breath. This pushing and pulling against the spikes was excruciating. Even worse, the flesh torn from their back by the flogging was scraped up and down against the rough wood of the post on which they hung. This gruesome cycle repeated itself over and over again: pushing and pulling on the spikes, grating the back up against the cross, a quick breath and then slumping down, scraping the back again as the lungs slowly filled with fluid. It is hard to imagine a more horrific death.

Hanging on the cross, victims experienced intense dehydration due to blood loss and exposure, evidenced by Jesus' pitiful cry, *"I'm thirsty."* This is a somber reminder Jesus set aside his divine nature to live a fully human life on earth, which means he was not shielded in any way from the full suffering of his crucifixion. And so, they lifted the common man's drink of sour wine to his dying lips with a sponge affixed to a hyssop branch. This same plant that was used by the Israelites to apply the blood of the lamb to their doorposts was now lifted to the one who would save them from death. (See Exodus 12:22.) As Jesus' life slipped away his final words were a declaration of triumph, *"It is finished."* Jesus had accomplished all he had come to do, finally completing the work John prophesied as the Lamb of God who takes away the sin of the world! (See John 1:29.)

Josephus tells us that some victims of crucifixion lasted for days on the cross, sometimes aided by a sharp seat meant to increase their pain and prolong their agony. Jesus had been beaten so badly he was severely weakened by the time he was hung on the cross. He was crucified around 9:00 AM, and by 3:00 PM he had died. (See Mark 15:25, 33.) Because the Passover officially began at sundown, along with the Sabbath, the religious leaders requested Pilate order the legs of the victims be broken to hasten their deaths. Once they could no longer push up with their legs, they would soon suffocate on their own fluids.

After breaking the legs of the two rebels who were crucified on either side of Jesus, the soldiers came to Jesus and saw he had already died and so did not break his legs, fulfilling the prophecy in Psalm 34:20. (See also Exodus 12:46.) To confirm their professional opinion, one of them pierced Jesus' side with his spear, and out flowed both blood and water, perhaps the bodily fluids in which he had drowned. This fulfilled another prophecy from Zechariah 12:10.

Jesus inaugurated the New Covenant in the water of the Jordan River and was now ratifying that same Covenant in the blood he shed on the cross. John points out these events are not something he heard about, but that he was an eyewitness to these very things. There was no question whether Jesus actually died or not because John saw it with his own eyes and knew it was true.

Jesus has accomplished what we could never do by offering himself as the perfect sacrifice for the sins of the world. What does it mean to you personally that Jesus suffered and died for you? How certain are you that it is true?

REFLECT AND RESPOND

What is Jesus saying to me right now?

What step of faith is Jesus calling me to take today?

FOOTSTEPS EVERY WEEK: REVIEW

Write a brief summary of what Jesus said to you each day this past week and the step of faith he called you to take:

MONDAY

TUESDAY

WEDNESDAY

THURSDAY

FRIDAY

SATURDAY

Footsteps Every Week: Reflect

Big Picture

As you look over what Jesus has said to you this past week, do you see any themes? What is the most important thing you need to remember and believe?

Predictable Pattern

As you look over what Jesus called you to do this past week, is there a new predictable pattern he is inviting you to establish in your life with God and others?

Plant the Word

As you look over the readings from this past week, write out the passage that feels most important for you and memorize it over the next week:

DAY 67

READ AND LISTEN: JOHN 19:38-42

Take a minute to listen for what God is saying in these verses…

COMMENT AND CONSIDER

John knew Jerusalem better than any of the other Gospel writers. He gives numerous geographical and political details which the historical and archaeological record has confirmed again and again. Here he gives us some clues about the place of Jesus' crucifixion and resurrection. He already told us the crucifixion was in a visible place *near the city.* (John 19:20) Now he tells us there was a garden cemetery with rock-cut tombs *in the place where he was crucified.* These details fit precisely with the location the first followers of Jesus identified as the rock of Golgotha and the tomb of Joseph of Arimathea, just outside the western city walls and only a stone's throw apart.

Today the Church of the Holy Sepulcher covers this ancient rock quarry-turned-cemetery and houses both the rock of Golgotha and the remains of the tomb. Although this location is now inside the walled city, archaeology has confirmed it was just outside the walls until ten years after Jesus' crucifixion. Between AD 41-43 Herod Agrippa I expanded the northwest walls of the city, enclosing the cemetery inside the walls. Here the early Christians of Jerusalem gathered each Sunday morning to celebrate the resurrection of Jesus for the next hundred years.

When Emperor Hadrian crushed the second Jewish Revolt in AD 135, he kicked all the Jews and Jewish Christians out of Jerusalem, erecting pagan Roman shrines over their religious sites. He filled in the rock quarry-turned-cemetery, built a large plaza over it, and placed a temple to Aphrodite, the goddess of sexual love, directly above the now-buried tomb of Joseph. Two hundred years later, after Emperor Constantine had converted to Christianity, he sent his mother Helena to build large churches in the most important places from Jesus' life.

When she asked the local Christians about these places, they told her the rock of Golgotha and the Tomb of Joseph were buried underneath the ruins of the temple of Aphrodite. Her workmen cleared away the rubble, dug down to the quarry, and amazingly found Golgotha and the empty tomb! If someone was going to make up the location of Golgotha and Joseph's tomb, they would never pick a place inside the walls and buried underneath a pagan temple. We have indisputable evidence that this is the actual place where Jesus was crucified and resurrected.

In this garden cemetery, Joseph of Arimathea had recently constructed a new tomb for his extended family. He was a member of the Sanhedrin, the ruling Jewish council of Jerusalem, and a man of means. Since the Messiah was to appear in Jerusalem to inaugurate the resurrection of the dead, Jerusalem was considered the best place to be buried. His friend Nicodemus was a Pharisee and also a member of the Sanhedrin. These two men of significant position and power had come to believe in Jesus and considered themselves his disciples, although they were hiding their relationship with him.

John tells us Nicodemus first came to Jesus under the cover of night to ask him spiritual questions. (See John 3:1-21.) Later, when the Sanhedrin was discussing how to condemn Jesus, Nicodemus stood up and said, *"Our law doesn't judge a man before it hears from him and knows what he's doing, does it?"* But the rest of the Council shouted him down. (See John 7:50-52.) Joseph and Nicodemus hid their connection with Jesus because it was politically dangerous for them to publicly identify themselves as his followers.

However, in the moment when it was most dangerous, immediately after Jesus had been executed as a traitor, they both stepped out of the shadows and into the light by asking Pilate for Jesus' body and burying him. Being identified with an executed rebel could easily lead to your own execution! But they decided there was no more room for hiding their faith. 75 pounds of myrrh and aloes was an extravagant amount to anoint a body. They were making an unmistakable statement about their devotion to Jesus.

How have you been hiding your faith in the shadows? What does it look like to boldly display your devotion to Jesus despite the risks?

Reflect and Respond

What is Jesus saying to me right now?

What step of faith is Jesus calling me to take today?

READ AND LISTEN: JOHN 20:1-9

Take a minute to listen for what God is saying in these verses…

COMMENT AND CONSIDER

First-century Jews who could afford it constructed elaborate rock-cut tombs to accommodate generations of an extended family. Typically, they had a low opening, leading into a chamber with burial shelves or deep slots cut into the rock walls, or sometimes both. Over time, new rooms were often added, resulting in extensive tombs with multiple burial chambers. The outer door was sealed either with a rectangular plug stone cut to the size of the opening or a disc-shaped rolling stone set into a sloped track that rolled down to block the door.

When someone died, the Jewish tradition was to bury them before the end of that same day. Recently a sealed first-century tomb was discovered in Jerusalem, preserving the grave clothes and confirming written accounts of Jewish burial practices. Normally, the body was taken to the tomb where it was carefully washed, anointed with perfume oil, and covered with aromatic spices to mask the smell of decay. Then it was wrapped lengthwise with a long linen shroud, leaving the face uncovered. A special cloth was placed over the face, and the entire body was wrapped with strips of cloth. Finally, the body was placed either on a stone burial shelf or slid into a burial slot inside the tomb. The opening was closed with the plug or rolling stone and sealed with clay to prevent odor from escaping.

On the first anniversary of the person's death, their extended family gathered at the tomb to remember and celebrate their loved one. The tomb was opened, and the bones of the deceased were gathered together and placed into an ossuary, a small stone box with a lid. The ossuary was then stored in the tomb with those who had died before them, awaiting the coming resurrection of the dead. Thousands of these first-century tombs and ossuaries have been discovered in and around Jerusalem.

The Gospel writers tell us Joseph of Arimathea had recently cut a new rolling-stone tomb in the ancient stone-quarry-turned-cemetery just outside the western walls of Jerusalem, near the rock of Golgotha. (See Matthew 27:60.) We can deduce this was still a single chamber tomb with a rock-cut shelf because Mary was able to bend over, look in through the outer door, and see two angels *sitting where Jesus's body had been lying, one at the head and the other at the feet.* (See John 20:11-12.) It was to this tomb Jesus' women disciples came early that Sunday morning.

Jesus was profoundly counter-cultural in his approach toward women. He publicly demonstrated their value and worth, from the highest to the lowest rungs of the social ladder. (See Mark 7:24-30, Matthew 9:18-26, and John 4:5-26.) He shockingly affirmed women as his disciples, for which there was no precedent in that society. (See Luke 8:1-3; 10:38-42.) When Jesus traveled to Jerusalem for his final Passover, *many* of his female disciples accompanied him and his twelve full-time male disciples. (See Matthew 27:55.) These women followed Jesus all the way to Golgotha to witness his brutal execution. These women watched as Joseph and Nicodemus sealed Jesus' body in the tomb. And these women ventured out to visit the tomb at their very first opportunity after the Passover Sabbath.

Mary Magdalene led the women disciples to show devotion to their Rabbi by re-anointing his body, but when they arrived at the cemetery, they were shocked to discover the tomb was empty! Assuming someone had stolen the body, Mary ran back to the upper room where the male disciples were still in hiding to report this terrible news. Peter and John raced to the garden cemetery and went inside to investigate the empty tomb. The grave clothes were still lying on the stone shelf, which did not fit the theory that Jesus' body had been stolen. Furthermore, there was something strange about how the linen wrappings were lying there and how the face cloth was carefully folded up and lying in a different place in the tomb. It was clear Jesus' body had not been stolen. But what actually happened?

How do you react when things happen that you can't explain? How do facts inform or detract from your faith?

REFLECT AND RESPOND

What is Jesus saying to me right now?

What step of faith is Jesus calling me to take today?

DAY 69

READ AND LISTEN: JOHN 20:10-18

Take a minute to listen for what God is saying in these verses…

COMMENT AND CONSIDER

Mary Magdalene was the leader of women disciples, so John focuses on her story although a group of women was there at the tomb. She came from Magdala, a city on the northwest shore of the Sea of Galilee, just west of Capernaum where Jesus centered his mission. Two first-century synagogues, along with a commercial district and some wealthy homes, have recently been discovered and excavated there. Although medieval writers associated Mary Magdalene with the sinful woman who anointed Jesus' feet during a banquet (see Luke 7:36-50), it is clear from Luke 8:2-3 that she was an aristocratic woman of means who helped support Jesus' mission financially, along with Joanna and Susanna, also upper-class women.

Jesus had delivered Mary Magdalene from the dehumanizing control of seven demons, a dramatic life transformation that planted a fierce devotion to her Rabbi into her heart. The fact that she led the other women disciples back to the tomb in the dark that early Sunday morning, knowing it was sealed by an enormous rolling stone and guarded by a squad of Roman soldiers, tells us she was a woman of great courage and determination.

However, Mary Magdalene's greatest hopes and dreams had been crushed when she saw Jesus breathe his final breath on the cross and heard the rolling stone slam shut on his tomb. Adding insult to injury, now it seemed the body of her Lord had been stolen, could be desecrated, and there was nothing she could do to stop it. It is no wonder she stood weeping outside the tomb. But something prompted Mary to stoop down and look back inside the tomb. Through her tears she saw something unbelievable: two brilliant angels sitting on either end of the stone shelf where Jesus' body had lain!

Disoriented, Mary Magdalene stood up, turned around, and saw a man standing there whom she assumed to be the cemetery gardener. He asked her why she was crying and what she was looking for. Mary answered, *"Sir, if you've carried him away, tell me where you've put him, and I will take him away.*" At that the risen Jesus simply spoke her name, *Mary.* Instantly she recognized him and cried out, *"Rabboni!"*—which means "my teacher." And then she fell at his feet and took hold of him, along with all the other women disciples, so Jesus had to tell them to let go! (See Matthew 28:9.) They were not going back to the way things used to be in Galilee. Jesus' resurrection was about to catapult them into a whole new life of mission by the power of the Spirit!

Their first assignment was to go to the male disciples and tell them this great good news of Jesus' resurrection. Mary Magdalene announced to the rest of the disciples, *"I have seen the Lord!"* This simple fact changed everything. She saw Jesus nailed to a cross and die, watched as his body was embalmed and sealed in a tomb, and then saw him gloriously transformed and made fully alive again. Jesus' resurrection means he was who he claimed to be, the fully human and fully divine, preexistent Son of God. It means everything he ever said was true, and he has the power to fulfill every promise he ever made. It means we are no longer in bondage to death!

In the patriarchal cultures of the ancient world, women were not generally considered reliable witnesses. In first-century Jewish society the testimony of women was not admissible in a trial. Celsus, a second-century Greek philosopher, dismissed the accounts of Jesus' resurrection because it was first reported by women. And yet John, like all the other male Gospel writers, records that the risen Jesus appeared first to Mary and the other female disciples. If someone in the first century were to fabricate a story about Jesus rising from the dead, they would never make women the primary witnesses! This important detail is another factor reflecting the historical reliability of the resurrection narratives.

What does the fact of Jesus' resurrection mean to you? Who are you going to tell this Good News?

REFLECT AND RESPOND

What is Jesus saying to me right now?

What step of faith is Jesus calling me to take today?

DAY 70

READ AND LISTEN: JOHN 20:19-23

Take a minute to listen for what God is saying in these verses…

COMMENT AND CONSIDER

Jesus had gone to great lengths to secure a large upper room where he and his closest disciples could share their final Passover meal before he was arrested. All historical and archaeological evidence points to the large courtyard home of Mary, the mother of John Mark and cousin of Barnabas, inside the city walls on the southwest hill of Jerusalem as the location of this house. When Jesus was arrested and his disciples scattered, it makes sense that many or all of them would have returned to this well-built, walled compound as their place of refuge. This home seemed to become the center for the movement of Jesus in Jerusalem during the months and years following his resurrection.

The disciples locked themselves in because they were terrified the religious leaders would continue their campaign to stamp out the movement Jesus began by arresting them and bringing them to Pilate for crucifixion as well. Despite the formidable defenses of this locked room in a secure stone house, the risen Jesus appeared unannounced in their midst. Based on this description, it would be easy to assume the risen Jesus was some kind of ethereal spirit, like a ghost, capable of passing through solid objects. Except Jesus made it a point to show them the wounds of crucifixion on his wrists and in his side. He showed them that he was the same person who had been nailed to the cross and that he still had a physical body, even though it was gloriously transformed in some mysterious way.

Luke records Jesus saying, *"Look at my hands and my feet, that it is I myself! Touch me and see, because a ghost does not have flesh and bones as you can see I have."* (Luke 24:39) The physical nature of the risen Jesus was clear when the women took hold of his feet and he had to tell them, *"Don't cling to me."* (See John 20:17.) The risen Jesus made it a point to eat fish with his disciples to prove he was real and physical. (See Luke 24:41-43.) This was not some kind of dream they were having. He was not a non-physical, spiritual apparition. This was not the product of wishful thinking or pious imagination. Jesus was transformed into a super-physical reality, the first fruits of the New Creation. It is not that Jesus had become an ethereal ghost; it is that solid stone walls were ethereal compared to the ultimate reality of Jesus' resurrected body. (See 1 Corinthians 15:35-49.)

When they saw this was really Jesus and he was really present and really alive, they were overjoyed! In the midst of that joy, Jesus gave them their new marching orders: *"As the Father has sent me, I also send you,"* then showed them the source of power that would guide and sustain their mission when he breathed on them the Holy Spirit. Jesus really did die on the cross as the perfect sacrifice of atonement. He really did rise from the dead, breaking the power of sin, hell, death, and the devil. This means now the gracious gift of forgiveness is available to all, and the separation between God and his people is coming to an end. Now the very Spirit of God dwells in the hearts and lives of his people!

Jesus' disciples received forgiveness for their sins, they were filled with the Spirit, and they answered Jesus' call to go out on mission just as he did, as they were sent all the way to the ends of the earth. Everywhere they went, they represented Jesus, doing what he did and declaring the Good News that through Jesus' death and resurrection all people can be set free from sin and empowered by the Spirit to live the life they were created to live. The disciples ("learners") were becoming apostles ("sent ones"), and through them this Good News of the Kingdom would literally change the course of human history.

Have you asked the risen Jesus to breathe his Holy Spirit into your heart and life? Have you accepted the call to bring this Good News and represent Jesus wherever you go?

REFLECT AND RESPOND

What is Jesus saying to me right now?

What step of faith is Jesus calling me to take today?

DAY 71

READ AND LISTEN: JOHN 20:24-31

Take a minute to listen for what God is saying in these verses…

COMMENT AND CONSIDER

Thomas' name means "The Twin" in Aramaic, and it is often translated into Greek to explain its meaning to Greek readers, implying it was actually a nickname. Thomas was not present that first Sunday evening when Jesus appeared to the other ten disciples in the upper room. He found it hard to believe Jesus could actually be alive despite their passionate testimony, *"We've seen the Lord!"* In response he gave the ultimatum, *"If I don't see the mark of the nails in his hands, put my finger into the mark of the nails, and put my hand into his side, I will never believe."* It is easy to disparage him as "Doubting Thomas," but it is important to remember all the others who believed in the risen Jesus had seen him and his wounds. For them, seeing was believing, and Thomas simply asked for the same.

The following Sunday, they were gathered in the upper room, and Jesus appeared to them again, but this time Thomas was there. Jesus did not condemn or even confront Thomas for his disbelief. All Jesus did was offer him exactly what he asked for: *"Put your finger here and look at my hands. Reach out your hand and put it into my side. Don't be faithless, but believe."* Thomas' response was a dramatic declaration of faith, *"My Lord and my God!"* Jesus' whole life was about making the invisible Father visible to the world, so it shouldn't surprise us that Jesus held out his arm and invited Thomas to put his finger in the nail marks on his wrists. Jesus was giving Thomas what he needed to believe.

Perhaps you feel a little bit like Thomas. Maybe you feel your faith would be stronger if you were actually there, seeing and hearing Jesus for yourself. But it is interesting that even some of those who saw the risen Jesus still had trouble believing in him. When the eleven remaining full-time disciples went to the mountain in Galilee where Jesus told them to meet, Matthew tells us *When they saw him, they worshiped, but some doubted.* (Matthew 28:17) Apparently seeing wasn't necessarily believing.

The English word "believe" is used to translate the Greek verb *pisteuo*, which is based on the same root as the word for "faith,"*pistis.* Since English doesn't have a verbal form of the word "faith," we translate it as "believe." But that word can be used to mean "agree with" rather than "exercise faith in." When Jesus invites Thomas to *believe*, he is challenging him to exercise faith and put his trust in him. We believe with our mind, but we trust with our heart and will. That is not to say our intellect has nothing to do with faith, but it is to say our mind can only take us so far. In the end we have to decide whether we are going to put our trust in Jesus by taking steps of faith.

The truth is you don't have to see Jesus physically in order to believe. Jesus told Thomas, *"Blessed are those who have not seen and yet believe."* The Apostle Paul says that faith comes by hearing the personal word of Jesus. (See Romans 10:17.) The role of the Apostles was to tell others what they had heard Jesus say and seen him do, so that faith would be planted in the hearts and minds of those who are open. This is exactly why John wrote this Gospel: *Jesus performed many other signs in the presence of his disciples that are not written in this book. But these are written so that you may believe that Jesus is the Messiah, the Son of God, and that by believing you may have life in his name.*

As you listen for the word Jesus is speaking to you right now, the Spirit is planting faith in your heart. The question is, will you keep listening and keep exercising that faith one step at a time? Thomas did, and it took him all the way to India to share the Good News with untold numbers of people! I wonder where that journey of faith will take you?

REFLECT AND RESPOND

What is Jesus saying to me right now?

What step of faith is Jesus calling me to take today?

DAY 72

READ AND LISTEN: JOHN 21:1-17

Take a minute to listen for what God is saying in these verses…

COMMENT AND CONSIDER

Simon Peter had failed spectacularly. Just as Jesus predicted, Peter sat by a charcoal fire in the courtyard of Caiaphas the High Priest and denied his Lord three times. (See John 18:15-27.) In all the Gospel accounts, there is no record of direct interaction between the risen Jesus and Peter up to this point. It is easy to imagine Simon, filled with shame over his failure, shuffling to the back of the group when the risen Jesus appeared, avoiding eye contact with him. Perhaps he no longer used the nickname Peter ("Little Rock") because he knew he had crumbled when the pressure was on. That may be why Simon decided to go back to fishing. He felt he was no longer qualified to be a full-time disciple, much less their leader.

These seven disciples fished all night and caught nothing, even though night was the best time to fish and they were professionals. At daybreak a stranger on the shore told them to put their nets down on the right side of the boat. That was the side with the steering oar, so usually the nets were let out on the left side of the boat. They were starting to remember another night when they caught nothing and got strange fishing advice. (See Luke 5:1-11.)

When they let down the nets on the wrong side of the boat, the lines suddenly pulled tight, and the nets were filled so full of large fish they couldn't even get them into the boat! Now memories of that other miraculous catch, the day Jesus called them to become full-time followers, came flooding back, and they all knew who was on the shore! Simon was so excited he tied his coat around his waist, jumped out of the boat, and swam to shore, leaving the others to drag in the loaded net full of fish.

Once Simon got to shore, his enthusiasm wavered. There is no mention of him approaching or addressing Jesus. His shame must have caught up with his excitement, reminding him he was a disqualified coward. When the others arrived, Jesus invited them all to join him for a breakfast of bread and grilled fish. As they sat there on the beach eating fish with Jesus, the smell of the charcoal fire brought Simon vivid memories of his failure. (See John 18:18.) Once they finished eating, Jesus addressed the elephant on the beach: *"Simon, son of John, do you love me more than these?"* Jesus was asking Simon if he loved him more than the fishing vocation to which he was planning to return.

Simon's response was immediate and clear: *"Yes, Lord, you know that I love you."* Simon was not returning to fishing because he preferred it to following Jesus, but because he had disqualified himself. Jesus' response was unexpected: *"Feed my lambs."* The prodigal son of the parable who had failed spectacularly never dreamed he would be welcomed back as a son but hoped he could return as a servant. (See Luke 15:19.) Simon felt the same way, that he would never be welcomed back as a shepherd, but just maybe he could be a sheep. Now Jesus was telling him to take the shepherd's role again.

Jesus asked the same question again. Simon's answer was the same, and Jesus' mandate was the same: *"Shepherd my sheep."* When Jesus asked the question a third time, the point was crystal clear: three denials, three reinstatements. It cut Simon deeply, but it was the pain of the surgeon's knife cutting away the dead tissue from a festering wound. Jesus loved Simon too much to gloss over or ignore his failure. He knew the only way Simon would ever be free of his guilt and shame was to address it head on with grace and truth. Simon was forgiven, healed, and restored. He loved Jesus far more than fishing, so he took his rightful role as shepherd of the sheep.

What failure has made you feel unworthy to represent Jesus? Do you love him? If so, he is calling you to be a sheep who is learning how to shepherd his sheep.

REFLECT AND RESPOND

What is Jesus saying to me right now?

What step of faith is Jesus calling me to take today?

FOOTSTEPS EVERY WEEK: REVIEW

Write a brief summary of what Jesus said to you each day this past week and the step of faith he called you to take:

MONDAY

TUESDAY

WEDNESDAY

THURSDAY

FRIDAY

SATURDAY

Footsteps Every Week: Reflect

Big Picture

As you look over what Jesus has said to you this past week, do you see any themes? What is the most important thing you need to remember and believe?

Predictable Pattern

As you look over what Jesus called you to do this past week, is there a new predictable pattern he is inviting you to establish in your life with God and others?

Plant the Word

As you look over the readings from this past week, write out the passage that feels most important for you and memorize it over the next week:

DAY 73

READ AND LISTEN: JOHN 21:18-25

Take a minute to listen for what God is saying in these verses…

COMMENT AND CONSIDER

Of the twelve full-time disciples, Peter and John became the two most influential leaders in the early church. They were fishermen from Capernaum whose families had formed a business partnership. They became part of Jesus' innermost circle of three disciples, along with John's brother, James. (See Mark 5:37, 9:2, 14:33.) Jesus sent Peter and John to prepare for their final Passover dinner with him in Jerusalem. (See Luke 22:8.) After Jesus' death and resurrection, they were going together to worship in the Temple when they healed the lame man at the Beautiful Gate. (See Acts 3:1-11.) Peter and John also went together to Samaria and ministered to those who had recently come to faith in Jesus. (See Acts 8:14-25.)

After John's brother, James was beheaded by Herod Agrippa I in Jerusalem, Peter and John were sent out from Jerusalem separately to continue spreading the Good News of Jesus across the Roman Empire. Peter went to Antioch, Asia Minor, and Corinth. Eventually he wrote a letter to the new churches in central Asia Minor (modern day Turkey) and ended up in Rome. (See 1 Peter 1:1.) According to the ancient accounts, Peter was crucified in Rome by Nero during the persecution that followed the great fire of AD 64.

Eventually John ended up in Ephesus, where he became the overseer of the most significant missional center in the early church. The churches of Ephesus planted many churches in western Asia Minor, and John's influence spread through the disciples he trained, such as Polycarp of Smyrna and Ignatius of Antioch. In Ephesus John wrote his Gospel and his three letters, probably in the AD 90s. As the youngest of the original twelve disciples, he lived the longest. According to ancient tradition, John is the only one of the twelve full-time disciples who was not martyred. Instead, he was exiled to the island of Patmos, off the western coast of modern Turkey, where he received the Revelation.

As we read John's Gospel, we see the growing competitiveness John felt toward Peter; at the last supper John says he was the one sitting beside Jesus in the honorable co-host's seat, while Peter was on the side of the table with less honor. (See John 13:23-24.) John mentions his connections that got him into the courtyard of the High Priest while Peter was refused entrance. (See John 18:15-16.) John tells us when they ran to the tomb on Easter morning, he outran Peter and got there first. (See John 20:4.) He says that when they saw the grave clothes arranged in the tomb, he was the one who believed, even though they still didn't fully understand. (See John 20:8-9.) When they returned to fishing, John tells us he was the one who first identified the stranger on the beach as Jesus. (See John 21:7.)

In the final passage of John's Gospel, we have another instance of this comparison between Peter and John. After Jesus restored Peter to his leadership role, he prophesied how Peter would be killed: *"…when you grow old, you will stretch out your hands and someone else will tie you and carry you where you don't want to go."* This is an obvious foretelling of Peter's eventual crucifixion in Rome. Jesus concluded this prophecy with the simple exhortation: *"Follow me."* But then John records Peter's comparative question, *"Lord, what about him?"* (referring to John). Jesus told Peter that was not his business and again exhorted him: *"Follow me."*

It is good to have role models who we can imitate, but it is easy to get caught up in comparing ourselves to each other and trying to gain God's approval by our accomplishments for him. Jesus tells us to simply focus on him, listen for his voice, and follow where he leads us one step of faith at a time. Are you comparing yourself in an unhealthy way to others? Are you trying to earn God's approval? How can you keep your focus on Jesus and continue to follow him one step of faith at a time?

REFLECT AND RESPOND

What is Jesus saying to me right now?

What step of faith is Jesus calling me to take today?

MORE RESOURCES BY BOB ROGNLIEN TO HELP YOU FOLLOW JESUS

Find them all at www.bobrognlien.com

❖ **Books** | *Footsteps Every Day: Matthew, Mark, Luke*
  ➢ Continue the journey you have begun with daily Gospel readings and reflections on the Way of Jesus, illuminated by insights from history, archaeology, and culture. These three books of daily devotions together with the current volume can take you through all four Gospels in one year.

❖ **Book** | *Recovering the Way: How Ancient Discoveries Help Us Follow the Footsteps of Jesus*
  ➢ An in-depth treatment of Jesus' life illuminated by the history of his time, the cultural background of his world, and archaeological discoveries from our time. Includes over 100 photos, reconstruction drawings, and maps. Excellent for serious students and teachers who want to go deeper.

❖ **Book** | *The Most Extraordinary Life: Discovering the Real Jesus*
  ➢ A shorter telling of the true story of Jesus from his baptism to his resurrection, informed by history, archaeology, and culture. Each chapter begins with an expanded account of an event from Jesus' life which reads like a historical novel. Written for everyday people who know Jesus and those who want to get to know him for the first time.

❖ **Video** | *Recovering the Way: The Video Series*
  ➢ An in-depth video teaching series that illuminates the life of Jesus with thousands of full color photos, reconstruction drawings, and animated maps. The twelve 45-minute episodes

correspond to the twelve chapters in the book *Recovering the Way* (see above) and will bring the Way of Jesus to life for you.

❖ **Trip |** *The Footsteps of Jesus Experience*
> ➤ A 14-day journey through Israel and Palestine, following the life of Jesus from birth to resurrection. We keep the group relatively small, stay in unique Christian guesthouses, drive ourselves in vans, do lots of walking off the beaten path, focus on historically verifiable sites, and keep an intentionally spiritual focus. It is not a tour, but an intensive pilgrimage.

❖ **Podcast |** *The Footsteps Podcast with Bob Rognlien and Matt Switzer*
> ➤ In each episode Footsteps Experience leaders Bob and Matt take you on a journey to a significant site in the Holy Land and show how the discoveries there bring a specific biblical passage to life with new insights and applications.

❖ **Trip |** *The Footsteps of Paul Experience*
> ➤ A 15-day journey from Antioch to Corinth through Turkey and Greece, following the missional journeys of the Apostle Paul and his disciples. We keep the group relatively small, stay in boutique hotels with historical and cultural charm, drive ourselves in vans, go off the beaten path, focus on the historically verifiable sites, and keep an intentionally spiritual focus. It is not a tour, but an intensive pilgrimage.

❖ **Book |** *A Jesus-Shaped Life: Discipleship and Mission for Everyday People*
> ➤ A practical guide to putting the Way of Jesus into practice in your everyday life with the people who are closest to you. It tells the story of how Bob and Pam learned to pattern their lives and their family more intentionally after Jesus. It also offers practical tools, vehicles, and strategies to make discipleship and mission a part of your daily life.

❖ **Book** | *Empowering Missional Disciples*

> ➢ A resource for leaders who want to help those they lead to live a life that looks more like Jesus and produces more of the fruit he produced. Includes lots of field-tested tools and vehicles for multiplying missional disciples.